The
Escontrias Family
Legacy:

A Very Personal Journey

Irma Escontrias Sanchez

Omega Press
El Paso, TX

THE ESCONTRIAS FAMILY LEGACY: A Very Personal Journey
COPYRIGHT © 2014 IRMA ESCONTRIAS SANCHEZ

OMEGA PRESS

An imprint of Omega Communications Group, Inc.

For information contact:

Omega Press

5823 N. Mesa, #839

El Paso, Texas 79912

Or http://www.kenhudnall.com

FIRST EDITION

Printed in the United States of America

DEDICATION

Each person leaves their lasting legacy in the world. My parents, Carlos and Maria Escontrias, gave me and my family unconditional love throughout our lives. I am constantly amazed when my family or friends talk about my parents and the wonderful memories they still have. We all learned from my parents' example and still carry lasting characteristics we learned from them. I dedicate this book to my parents in the hope that generations to come will know all about their wonderful family.

I would like to thank everyone who has supported me in making this book a reality. I appreciate all of my family, friends, and the wonderful institutions who have contributed to the contents of this book. I would also like to thank all of my family and friends who have attended our special family functions throughout the years. I look forward to the new memories we will all make as we continue through our path in life and hope you are inspired to write your own book.

TABLE OF CONTENTS

Beautiful Hueco Tanks today

Figure 1: Hueco Tanks was once the home of the Escontrias Family as well as the site of the Old Butterfield Station

Figure 2: Picture reprinted from the collection of the Texas Parks and Wildlife Department

Introduction

The Escontrias family legacy is one rich in history. A legacy is something you leave behind. This book is dedicated to my family in honor of all they have left behind in the form of what they have taught us. Many times we think that those we love will live forever and that we have all the time in the world to record family stories. I will forever regret not taking more time to record our family history. I have learned that each person is a living book filled with endless stories….a virtual wealth of information.

My hope is that some of our oral history will be recorded in this book and that our history will live on forever in the generations to come. This book contains stories handed down from generations gathered from the personal memories of my parents. Thus, this book is dedicated to my parents, Carlos and Maria Escontrias, who will live on forever in our memories. Carlos and Maria were the best parents anyone could ask for and they will live forever in my heart.

I would like to thank the following individuals and institutions who contributed to this book:

Jaime Sanchez

Cassandra Nicole Sanchez

Jaime Antonio Sanchez

Mary Alice Tellez

Beatrice Morales

Patricia Castaneda

Wanda Olszewski

El Paso Community College

Socorro Independent School District

Texas Parks and Wildlife Department

**Figure 3: Escontrias ranch home picture reprinted from the
collection of the Texas Parks and Wildlife Department**

**Figure 4: Escontrias ranch picture reprinted from the collection of
the Texas Parks and Wildlife Department**

**Figure 5: Former Escontrias family home located at Hueco Tanks
State Park**

Hueco Tanks State Park was once the home and ranch
of the Escontrias family.   Our family has countless
memories and stories of life on the ranch.   The original
Escontrias family home is still located on the grounds of
the Hueco Tanks State Park and serves as the Hueco Tanks
Interpretive Center.   Our family has donated family
pictures which are located in the center. The Interpretive
Center is open to the public and is filled with information
and memorabilia.

Figure 6: Family pictures donated to Hueco Tanks are located in the Interpretive Center

Figure 7: Escontrias family home at Hueco Tanks. Picture reprinted from the collection of the Texas Parks and Wildlife Department

Figure 8: View of the Escontrias Home as it stands today at Hueco Tanks

Figure 9: Hueco Tanks in the days of Escontrias Family ownership. This area of the ranch was known as El Tanque de la Virgen

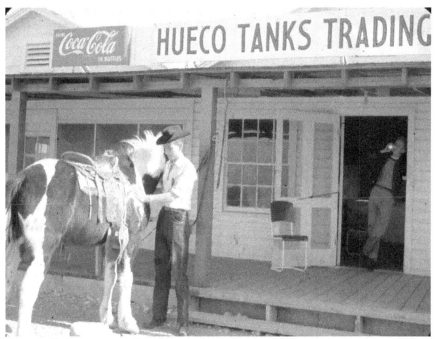

Figure 10: Picture reprinted from the collection of the Texas Parks and Wildlife Department

Chapter 1
My Grandparents
Silverio and Pilar Escontrias

I never had the honor of meeting my grandparents, Silverio and Pilar Escontrias. My mother was pregnant with me when my grandmother passed away and my grandfather had already passed away twenty-nine years prior to my birth. The information I know about my grandfather was attained through family stories and research.

I wish I could have met my grandfather.....a true trailblazer in every sense of the word. My grandfather was born in Tularosa, New Mexico. He came to El Paso when he was fifteen years old. My grandmother Pilar's family were Spaniards who migrated from San Antonio, Texas and settled in San Elizario, Texas. My grandparents were married at San Felipe and were the parents of eleven children. Juan, Manuela, Filberta, Jose, Pedro, Ramon, Silverio, Santiago (Jim), Fredencia, Ramon II, and Carlos....all deceased. I only know about some of the birth locations for my uncles and aunts. Tio (Uncle) Santiago and Tio (Uncle) Jose were born at the Escontrias ranch which is now Hueco Tanks. My dad, Carlos, Tio (Uncle) Ramon, Tio (Uncle) Silverio Jr. and Tio (Uncle) Pedro were born at the Socorro farm.

My grandfather was a Texas Ranger when you didn't see Hispanics in that role. He also served as a deputy sheriff in the county. An El Paso Herald Post newspaper article dated July 13, 1910, stated that "several Mexicans throughout the county, some of them engaged in the employment business and others in ranching, hold commissions to carry revolvers. The list of one hundred fifty seven Deputy Sheriffs in El Paso County included my grandfather, Silverio Escontrias. In another El Paso Herald

Post newspaper article, date July 21, 1920 my grandfather's name was on the list of deputies whose commission had expired which indicates that he served as a Deputy Sheriff for ten years. He also served as a trustee on the board of the Socorro Independent School District.

My grandfather's gifts to needy families, his church, and education were numerous. He donated land which was used to build the Escontrias Elementary School. He also donated land to La Purisima Catholic Church in Socorro, Texas. He believed in family, law and order. He was also an excellent horseman, and I discovered many newspaper articles citing his times for roping and steering contests. According to the October 24, 1907 newspaper article in the El Paso Herald Post, his roping time was 2:20. In another article dated July 5, 1909, his time in the second steer contest was 1:18.

In 1898, Silverio Escontrias acquired Hueco Tanks and turned it into a ranch. The Escontrias family operated Hueco Tanks until 1956 charging a small fee for visitors who came to enjoy the scenic area. My grandparents and their family resided at Hueco Tanks for over fifty years. In the mid-1960's, El Paso County acquired Hueco Tanks and began operating it as a county park. On June 12th, 1969, the county gave Hueco Tanks by special deed to the Texas Parks and Wildlife Department.

My grandfather passed away at his home on September 16th, 1932. His last words were: "I'm going to rest now, and see Pete." Apparently, my Uncle Pete was accidently shot and died at the farm four years before my grandfather died. In an El Paso Herald Post newspaper article dated July 17, 1928, I discovered that my Uncle Pedro Escontrias was twenty-six when he was accidentally killed at the Socorro home. Apparently, my Uncle Jim thought the pistol he was playing with was useless and the pistol accidentally discharged while the two waited for dinner. My grandfather also said "I want you all to be good children and be careful." My grandfather died surrounded by his family.

As I have learned more about my grandfather, I can only be proud of the legacy he has left behind. He left his legacy etched in his family and his generosity has resulted in the education of future generations.

Figure 11: Escontrias Family Portrait

Figure 12: Silverio Escontrias   **Figure 13: Pilar Loya Escontrias**

Figure 14: Silverio and Pilar Escontrias

Figure 15: Silverio and Pilar Escontrias

Figure 16: Pilar Escontrias and family

Figure 17: Pilar Escontrias and family

Figure 18: Pilar Escontrias and family

Figure 19: Pilar Escontrias holding Carlos Escontrias

Figure 20: Pilar Escontrias

Figure 21: Pilar Escontrias surrounded by her family

Figure 22: Pilar Escontrias and family

Figure 23: Pilar Escontrias and family

Figure 24: Pilar Escontrias and family members

Figure 25: Pilar Escontrias and family members

Figure 26: Silverio Escontrias, Texas Ranger, with a friend

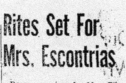

Rites Set For Mrs. Escontrias

Rosary services for Mrs. Pilar Escontrias, who died Saturday, were to be held at 8 p. m. today in the Harding and Orr Montana Avenue Chapel.

Mrs. Escontrias was a lifelong resident of the El Paso area. She and Mr. Escontrias lived for more than 50 years on their ranch which included Hueco Tanks. After the death of Mr. Escontrias in 1932, Mrs. Escontrias continued to be active in ranching.

Funeral Mass will be said tomorrow at 10 a. m. in the Socorro Catholic Church. The Rev. Zuniga will officiate.

Pallbearers will be Sheriff Bob Bailey, Alex Gonzales, Jack Black, Felipe Duran, Mike Apodaca, C. P. Brown and Russell Menzie.

Honorary pallbearers will be George Bovee, L. A. Campbell, Tom Shioji, Sid Ashley, Tony Apodaca, Simon McVey, Harvey Hilley, Jim Carr, J. R. Davis, L. M. Jones, Tomas Cardenas, Mike Sullivan, Max Foster, Wallace Fields, Sterling Roberts, Ben Cook, Calvert Tucker, Hugh Mc-

Pioneer EP Woman Dies At 84

MRS. P. L. ESCONTRIAS

Mrs. Pilar L. Escontrias, 89 of Ysleta, died Saturday in a local hospital. She was a life long resident of El Paso, having been born at San Elizario, and was the widow of the late Silverio Escontrias, former deputy sheriff, Texas Ranger and prominent rancher and farmer.

The family of Mrs. Escontrias were Spaniards who migrated in this area, including the Hueco Tanks area, where they resided for over 50 years. After Mr. Escontrias died in 1932, Mrs. Escontrias continued to be active in ranching until ill health forced her retirement.

She was a member of the Socorro Catholic Church, the Sacred Heart Society, the Immaculate Conception Society and the Altar Society.

Survivers include two daughters, Mrs. Manuel E. Apodaca and Mrs. Fidencia E. Aguirre; five sons, Juan Escontrias, S. L. Escontria, Ramon Escontrias, Charles Escontrias and Silver A. Escontrias, a sister Mrs. Loretto Zuniga; a brother, Pedro Loya, both of Los Angeles, California, 23 grandchildren, and 25 great-grandchildren all whom are in El Paso for the funeral.

Rosary services will be held at 8 p. m. Monday in the Harding and Orr Montana Chapel. Funeral mass will be said at 10 a. m. Tuesday in the Socorro Catholic Church with the Rev. Zuniga, officiating.

Burial will be in Evergreen Cemetery.

Figure 27: Pilar Escontrias' Obituary

'Be Good Children,' Says E. P. Pioneer on Death Bed

Silverio Escontrias Smiles as End Comes; Tells Sons, Daughters He Is "Going to Rest Now"

"I'm going to rest now, and to see Pete. I want you all to be good children—and be careful."

Silverio Escontrias, pioneer El Pasoan, uttered these words to his children gathered around his bedsid shortly before he died at the family residence, Socorro.

"Father's voice was quiet and soft as he spoke to us," said Juan Escontrias, a son. "He seemed happy at the prospect of seeing Pete, my brother, who was accidentally shot at the farm four years ago.

"Pete was the only one missing from the family circle around father's bed. Father talked about Pete and the rest in store for him all during those last few hours. He kept us near him until he died quietly."

Funeral services for Escontrias will be held at the Socorro mission at 9 a. m. tomorrow. Burial will be in Evergreen.

Escontrias was born at Tularosa, N. M. 60 years ago. He came to the El Paso valley when he was 15. Later he bought the H Tanks ranch. For 35 years he a deputy sheriff in the county.

Escontrias rode with his men on his ranch until doctors advised him last year to leave the saddle.

His gifts to needy families and to his church were numerous. He gave the county land on which the Escontrias school was built in Socorro.

Escontrias is survived by his widow, six sons, Juan, Jim, Joe Silverio Jr., Ramon and Charlie Escontrias, and three daughters, Mrs. Fidencia Aguirre, Mrs. Feliberta Marquez and Mrs. Manuel Apodaca.

Figure 28: Silverio Escontrias' Obituary

Chapter 2
Hueco Tanks History from Ranch to Park

Figure 29: Cattle roaming at the Escontrias Ranch

**Figure 30: Hueco Tanks photo reprinted with permission of the
Texas Parks and Wildlife Department**

Land ownership has long been the focus of much strife and debate. Great empires have spread over several continents. Conquerors decimated native peoples and claimed their lands. They, in turn, were conquered by invaders from other lands. So, who owns the land? And for how long?[1]

The spectacular rock formation known as Hueco Tanks, thirty miles from El Paso, has caused this question

---

[1] "Escontrias Ranch: A Link to Hueco Tanks Park by Lorraine Kress with additional research by Brenda Palma" Reprinted with permission from Borderlands, a student research and writing project of the English Department at El Paso Community College, El Paso, Texas, Ruth E. Vise, Faculty Advisor and Editor. All rights reserved.

to be asked in recent history. Hueco Tanks is named for the unique hollows (huecos), or "tanks," in the rocks which collect and store rainwater, creating an oasis in the southwestern desert. Ancient native cultures gave way to the influence of white men, who began to claim the land as theirs.

Based on Folsom projectile points which have been found there, evidence shows that bison hunters inhabited Hueco Tanks about 10,000 years ago. With the extinction of the bison came people of the Desert Archaic Culture, who lived in pit houses partially underground, some 3,000 to 6,000 years ago.

Later, the Jornada Mogollon Culture left distinct markings on the rocks dating to 1000 C.E. Hueco Tanks employee Wanda Olszewski said in an interview with this writer that most of the paintings and carvings on the rock surfaces at Hueco Tanks are from this ancient culture. More modern inhabitants of the tanks have included the Mescalero and Lipan Apaches and perhaps the Jumano Indians. The Kiowas and Comanches knew the area, and El Paso's Tigua Indians still claim the area as sacred ground.

The Mescalero Apaches used the tanks frequently in the 18th and 19th centuries. It was an ideal refuge from their enemies, Spaniards, Mexicans and American. Historian C.L. Sonnichsen wrote about a Spanish campaign against the Mescaleros in 1775 in which they were defeated. Another campaign was launched the following year that drove most Apaches even further west, while one band stayed behind in the tanks.

With the California Gold Rush, travelers through Hueco Tanks were more and more often non-native adventurers and settlers heading west. The tanks became a rest and water stop for both humans and animals. In 1858, the Butterfield Overland Mail even established a stagecoach stop there, but it moved the following year to a more protected location. Some of the history of Hueco Tanks was lost at that time when waiting stagecoach passengers marked over the pictographs created by earlier cultures and left their names and dates as well as drawings.

In 1898, Silverio Escontrias purchased Hueco Tanks and the family operated their cattle business from an adobe ranch house. This signified the first documented purchase of the property. However, in an unpublished paper, historic preservation consultant Terri Myers stated that in 1885, Juan Armendariz, possibly a godfather to Silverio Escontrias, first acquired the land through the establishment of the Corporation of Socorro by the Pueblo de Socorro Grant. That same grant also awarded some of the land to the Texas and Pacific Railway company, from which Silverio Escontrias made his purchase.

Silverio Escontrias was a Texas Ranger, well-versed in the establishment of law and order. Jim Escontrias said in a 1984 interview with El Paso Herald-Post columnist, Virginia Turner that Silverio Escontrias "always got along well with the Indians. They'd trade horses."

Ranching in such an isolated area gave raiding Indians an easy target, so Escontrias relied on his powers of communication to secure peace. The accessibility of water greatly outweighed the risk of raids. In the same interview, the younger Escontrias remembered the family and cattle getting all of their water from Hueco Tanks. The Escontrias family owned and operated the cattle ranch until 1956.

Terri Myers' research also revealed plans that date back to 1885 for Hueco Tanks to be turned into a resort, but when Armendariz acquired the land, the plans were put on the back burner. Escontrias eventually began to charge curious visitors a small admission fee. Visitors freely roamed the area until careless hunters endangered the cattle, resulting in the cessation of public access. Instead, special passes were issued to parties to help monitor people on the land.

Local newspaper articles report that on July 22, 1935, the Escontrias family offered to sell a portion of the land to the county for $42,000 to develop a park, but the purchase depended on a tax levy. Another article a few days later said that "protests against purchase of Hueco Tanks by the county, particularly at the price set by the Escontrias family, are piling into the office of Judge Joseph McGill." The purchase did not take place, and new plans for development surfaced. The plans included housing developments, lakes, a frontier-town movie set, golf courses, a resort and restaurants. The plans were never put into effect.

It is unclear who owned the land following the Escontrias family, but El Paso County acquired it in the mid-1960's. On June 12, 1969, the county then gave Hueco Tanks, by exclusive deed, to the Texas Parks and Wildlife Department. In May 1970, Hueco Tanks Historical Park was officially opened to the public.

Over the years, before and even after Hueco Tanks became a park, visitors defaced rocks with graffiti and vandalized priceless pictographs. Graffiti removal is a slow, laborious, and expensive task, with one such removal costing $10,000. Care must be taken to preserve the integrity of the rock and the painting or carving. Today, access to Hueco Tanks is severely restricted. One of the park's major concerns is to educate the public to respect the land in order to preserve the historical paintings and carvings.

But the story does not end there. Hueco Tanks evidently has been a sacred site for centuries for various tribes, including the Tiguas of Ysleta. In his book, Historic El Paso, Ken Flynn wrote that "excavations of pit houses identified as belonging to the Mogollon, from whom the Pueblo Indians are descended, indicate the use of a 'kiva' or 'tula,' a special ceremonial room used for prayer and sacrifice to the gods." What others call rock art, the Tiguas call spiritual and historical symbols. The Tiguas see Hueco Tanks as their ancestral home and consider sacred many specific sites.

In 2000, a consulting firm for the Tiguas prepared a management plan for Hueco Tanks addressing many topics such as limited public access, desecration of sacred shrines as cultural resources, imposed religious infringements on culturally affiliated peoples and others. These are issues between the Texas Parks and Wildlife Department and the Tiguas, and they remain unresolved. The document, prepared by Cultural Consultants, is available at the downtown El Paso Public Library.

The Escontrias Ranch represented a unique bridge between Indian cultures and state ownership. This family lived off the land and moved on, as other cultures have done for thousands of years. Today, the Escontrias ranch house still stands and is used as an Interpretive Center for visitors to Hueco Tanks.

Chapter 3
Family Stories from Hueco Tanks

Figure 31: Carlos Escontrias and the ranch hand believed to be Felix

Hueco Tanks was once the Escontrias family ranch. My one regret is that I did not record more stories. But, years ago, I went over one evening and caught my Mom and Dad (Carlos and Maria Escontrias) in a story telling mode. Here are some of the stories they shared:

My father, Carlos Escontrias, told me that Billy the Kid, a notorious outlaw, carved his name on one of the rocks while hiding out in the caves at Hueco Tanks. I was also told about an Indian legend, believed in the community, which declares that a large deposit of gold was left in Hueco Tanks by the Spaniards. My grandfather, Silverio Escontrias, tried for many years to persuade the Indians to reveal the hiding place of the gold but without success. Legend also has it that a hermit, who used to live in a cave, left Hueco Tanks one night carrying a load of what appeared to be heavy boxes. According to the story, the old hermit was found murdered while enroute to Las Cruces and the boxes were never found.

A story told to my father by my Grandma Pilar was that one day it was raining cats and dogs. The water was so high it was getting in through one door and out the other. In order for the crib not to float away, my grandfather, Silverio, tied the crib to the bed. On that memorable day, my grandmother Pilar gave birth to my Tio (Uncle) Santiago.

I was also told that the family house at Hueco Tanks burned and one entire room was destroyed. The Hueco Tanks house was smaller than the family home in Socorro. Therefore, Uncle Ramon also took an Army barracks building to the ranch for the extended family to stay in.

One day, Mom (Maria Escontrias) and Tia (Aunt) Chavela were charging for cars to come into the ranch. At that time, it was a fifty cent charge. Business was really slow, so Mom and Tia (Aunt) Chavela decided to go to the area called the San Ramon tank. Our family always had rifles with them to protect against snakes and wild animals such as mountain lions and coyotes. The snakes shed their skin every year and Mom and Tia (Aunt) Chavela found the skin on the floor. Mom told Tia (Aunt) Chavela, "Are you prepared to find this snake?" Tia (Aunt) Chavela said she was ready. They made sure they had bullets in their 22 caliber rifles.

Once the snake was located, both Mom and Tia (Aunt) Chavela shot at the snake and thought it was dead. They put some dirt in the trunk of the car. They then went to look for a stick to grab the snake and placed the snake in the trunk because they wanted to show it to my Dad who was roping at the Rough Riders. They told my Dad, "Look what we killed!"

When they opened the trunk, the snake was still very much alive. Dad almost died from shock. He told my Mom to cut off the head of the snake next time since the snake had cured himself in the dirt.

November was a time for deer hunting. Apparently, Tio (Uncle) Juan really liked to hunt. During the hunting season the family would make breakfast on an open fire. They would eat eggs, bacon, sausage, chorizo, and "papas" (potatoes). There was no charge to the public for deer hunters who would come to the ranch. Mom said the family would cook for the hunters. They used to cook outside on an open fire by the Acebushi right past the tank. Mom told me about a time the family brought a huge truck filled with goats. Unfortunately, the family would see the campers cooking goats on the grill. The goats disappeared quickly and didn't get a chance to reproduce.

I was also told about a time when the area known as El Cerro Alto was losing cattle and sheep. Dad followed the trail of a mountain lion. Thank goodness, he never located the mountain lion.

Dad, my Tio (Uncle) Jose, my Tio (Uncle) Ramon, and one of the ranch hands, Felix, roped a big 14 point deer. They took the deer to the ranch and placed hay in the corral to feed him. The deer wouldn't move, drink water, or eat and would not raise his head. Dad and uncles tried to let the deer go, but he wouldn't budge or even charge at them. The deer was in shock and died a week or so later.

Tio (Uncle) Juan, Tio (Uncle) Jose and Dad would go to school in Socorro and then spend one or two months working at the ranch in the summer. The family weddings would take place at the Socorro house. The family had army barracks at the ranch and this was where my parents would stay.

My parents told me stories of lots of "cantadores" (singers)....singing around an open fire....and great memories. Mom recalled beautiful times roaming the areas which are now protected areas of the park. My sisters, Patty, Licha and Bea would run all over the ranch. We weren't afraid and we were very lucky no one in the family has ever been hurt climbing the amazing mountains.

Another story I was told was about Juan Flores who was supposedly followed by someone on a horse and the horse came to a stop on the left side of the "Tanque de la Virgen" (Tank of the Virgen). Juan was told that someone was buried along there. An old Indian told him there was a cemetery there. According to legend, Indians had to be buried standing up. Dad, Uncle Ramon and the ranch hands started digging and found a skeleton. Dad brought the skull home and then couldn't sleep. Mom was going crazy seeing that skull even with her eyes closed. She asked them to bury it in the same place where they had found it. They took it back and buried it in the same place.

My parents recalled family parties, Bar B Q's, plentiful food which included "costillas de rez" (spare ribs). There was no electricity so the family would cook outside on an open fire or in the kitchen using a wooden stove. During family gatherings, the family would catch Tepocate (fish-like creatures) and throw them back in. The family also enjoyed swimming in the lake. There were snakes so you had to be careful. When they were out riding horses, you had to be careful with the huge holes made by the prairie dogs. The fear was that the horses would trip and fall. Prairie dogs also indicated a change of weather. Dad's horse tripped once, and both my Dad and the horse were lucky to not get hurt. Actually, we are grateful that Dad never had a serious accident. He would also ride his horse across a narrow. In thinking about all of these family memories, I know my Dad was a gifted horseman.

The family hired a full-blooded Indian named Felix who also served as a guide. Felix would also translate the writings on the wall. Mom, Dad and Tia (Aunt) Chavela were following Felix. They were all looking for a green tree in the rocks which housed a place they called the Vineyard. The Vineyard was filled with beautiful wild vines and poisonous wild grapes. Once they passed The Vineyard, they kept climbing up a mountain toward a cave. They all got to the cave and Felix went in first. He slithered into the cave like a snake. However, he was afraid to go any further. They were looking for a spring that was supposed to have had gold. Felix thought he was close to the spring and thought he could see "un ojo de agua" (an eye of water) at the top of the cave. But he got scared and stopped going into the cave. The Indians had blocked the passage with plaster and rocks. They had also cleaned the Tinaja (a waterhole in the rocks), and used it for pottery. They all tried to find out where the water was coming from. To this day, they did not find out where the water was coming from.

There were also lots of mysteries associated with the ranch. During this time, the Army was using uranium. A ranch hand had discovered a vein of uranium. According to my parents, there had been dynamite taken from Los Reynosos. The family dynamited the area and made a huge hole. The uranium veins were thick and beautiful. Dad and

Uncle Ramon brought down some of the uranium-filled rocks. They both went to the plaza in downtown El Paso to check what it was worth. They were told that the rocks contained uranium. They were also told that even if they were millionaires, they wouldn't be able to get it out. These rocks couldn't be hauled out on trucks. They would need a railroad. According to my family, the uranium is still there, but who knows where?

Dad and Tio (Uncle) Ramon were very daring when it came to their land. They planted cotton and it grew. However, the jack rabbits would eat the cotton. They eventually had to admit defeat and take a tractor to clear the area.

There was a cave known as La Cueva de Guano or La Jaria. This cave was full of guano, also known as bat doodoo. The family used this as a fertilizer for the ranch.

In researching the book, I was able to find a series of El Paso Herald Post newspapers articles which gave me more insight into the life of my family.

In an article in the El Paso Herald Post dated May 5, 1911, there was a case in County Court with A.S.J. Eylar presiding. Apparently, E. Garcia was charged with threatening to kill my grandfather, Silverio Escontrias and he was found not guilty by the jury.

Apparently, there were many problems with visitors throughout the time of ranch ownership. In an El Paso Herald Post newspaper article dated April 29, 1915, there was a formal announcement of the closing of Hueco Tanks to visitors by my grandfather, Silverio Escontrias. The order was justified by the "abuse of privileges" of which visitors have been continually guilty. Several head of valuable stock had died of thirst because of being run away from the watering places by campers shooting in the vicinity and frightening them. The gates had been often left open by autoists which permitted the stock to escape or mix with other stock and this interfered greatly with the operation of the ranch.

Years later, records indicated that my grandfather still faced many problems in trying to manage a ranch of that size. According to an August 24, 1925 article in the El Paso Herald Post newspaper, my grandfather decided to put up a no trespassing sign which was backed by the County Authority. In the article, my grandfather stated that parties and individuals were coming out to his property at all times and committing depredations for which he wasn't going to stand any longer. Judge McClintock made the statement that he and the officers of El Paso County would stand "right square behind Mr. Escontrias in protecting his property."

Apparently, unknown parties came onto the ranch, brought guns, and in shooting around the premises, they killed his best cow and horse. Unknown parties visited The Tanks, and one member carried a .22 caliber rifle. A dispute arose among them as to whether a .22 caliber rifle bullet would penetrate the hide of a fine bull he had on his ranch. In order to settle the dispute, the owner of the rifle took a "crack" at the bull's stomach with the result that the bullet not only penetrated the hide but killed the fine and valued animal.

My grandfather stated "Not only do they shoot my stock, but drinking parties frequently come out to The Tanks, and when they empty a bottle, they throw the broken remains into one of the tanks, and my stock, sometimes wading in them, severely cut their feet on the glass. But the climax came the other day when someone visited my tanks, unplugged one of them, and let thousands and thousands of gallons of valuable water run out and soak up in the sand and absolutely wasted the water. After much work, I had planned a series of tanks, one following the other along a small stream of water, and by these tanks, I manage to conserve a years' water supply for my stock, which would otherwise perish for the want of it."

My grandfather said that in order to stop such vandalism, he was going to build an expensive wire fence around his property, and if that didn't stop marauders, he was going to employ a special officer who would be commissioned from the county to stand guard over it, and arrest anyone who tried to enter.

In the article, my grandfather stated, "The other day, I was out at one of the tanks, when a party came out. I told them no one was allowed to enter unless they had permission from the owner. A lady said, "Why, that's all right. We know Mr. Escontrias, and he gave us a pass." My grandfather said "Let me see your pass." She said, "Oh, I have lost it; but it will be all right." My grandfather asked her when she saw Mr. Escontrias and she said, "Oh, I saw him yesterday, and he gave me the pass then." My grandfather stated that he still let her pass because he couldn't insult a lady!

In an El Paso Herald Post article dated July 2, 1952, Juan Escontrias said, "The Hueco Tanks area is open on Sundays." My grandmother, Pilar Escontrias, set the price of admission at one dollar per car.

Hueco Tanks will always hold memories, each priceless to the bearer. Mom's memories include living a life with a lot of family members. Dad's memories include living the life of a cowboy…. riding horses and chasing cattle. For my sisters and me, Hueco Tanks brings memories of Easter gatherings and all the fun of a picnic. We would chase after our cousins and would encounter the added problems of either keeping up or being left behind.

For those who visit Hueco Tanks, you will have the ability to enjoy rock climbing and looking at the pictographs. You are able to visit a state park filled with lots to do, see and enjoy. I am grateful for the Hueco Tanks staff who are dedicated to preserving what was once our family's ranch for generations of visitors to come.

Once we are all long gone, the beauty and wonder of Hueco Tanks will live on. It is only fitting to know that generations to come will see this, the former Escontrias home, at Hueco Tanks and wonder about the lives of the people who once lived there.

Figure 32: Cowboys at Hueco Tanks

Figure 33: Mary Alice Tellez and Rosaline Duran

Figure 34: Carlos Escontrias taking in the sun

Figure 35: Mary Alice Tellez

**Figure 36: Carlos Escontrias and the Cedillos Brothers from
Monticello, New Mexico**

Figure 37: Family ranch photo

Figure 38: Maria Escontrias with Robert and Enriqueta Armendariz

Figure 39: Maria Escontrias and friends

Figure 40: Carlos and Mary Escontrias with Inez Armendariz

Figure 41: Family members at Escontrias Ranch

Figure 42: Family members at Escontrias Ranch

Figure 43: Family members at Escontrias Ranch

Figure 44: Family members at Escontrias Ranch

Figure 45: Family members at Escontrias Ranch

Figure 46: Family Members at Escontrias Ranch

Figure 47: Family members at Escontrias Ranch

Figure 48: Family children at Escontrias Ranch

Figure 49: Family members at Escontrias Ranch

Figure 50: Family members at Escontrias Ranch

Figure 51: Enjoying a picnic at the Escontrias Ranch

Figure 52: Working at the Escontrias Ranch

Figure 53: Working at the Escontrias Ranch

Figure 54: A new foal born on the Escontrias Ranch

Figure 55: Ranch hand believed to be Felix

Figure 56: Mary Alice Tellez and friend

Figure 57: Charlie Armendariz

Figure 58: Carlos Escontrias and his horse "Barrozo"

Figure 59: Escontrias family ranch photo

Figure 60: Escontrias family ranch photo

Figure 61: Cattle roaming freely at the Escontrias Ranch

Chapter 4
Escontrias Family Farm in Socorro, Texas

Figure 62: Escontrias family farm in Socorro, Texas

Our family still owns the family home in Socorro, Texas. My grandfather supervised the production of cotton and alfalfa on the farm. The original house is approximately one hundred years old. My father was born in that home and my sisters and I grew up there. Once my father suffered a stroke, he began to sell sections of the farm. Today, only the family home remains.

Figure 63: Escontrias family home in Socorro, Texas

Figure 64: Escontrias family home in Socorro, Texas

Figure 65: Escontrias family home in Socorro, Texas as it stands today

Chapter 5
Escontrias Elementary School and
the History of Donated Land

Figure 66: Socorro School renamed Escontrias Elementary School

Socorro, Texas had its beginnings in 1680 when a group of Spanish settlers were driven out of the Santa Fe area by the Pueblo Indian revolt. The Spanish settlers established the San Pedro de Alcantero settlement seventeen miles from El Paso on October 13, 1680. The settlement was later renamed Socorro, after the original Socorro Spanish Land Grant[2].

According to Nancy Lee Hammons, author of a master's thesis entitled "A History of El Paso County to 1900," the first school in Socorro and Ysleta opened in 1878 at Martin's Ranch, three miles from Ysleta. In 1885, a school census compiled by the county Assessor listed fifteen males and sixty-eight females in the Socorro district between the ages of eight and fifteen.

In 1906, there was a boy's school and a girl's school on Socorro road. The buildings were adobe structures. In 1918, the school was moved to a one-room building located near what is now North Loop and Buford road. Board members William O'Shea and Silverio Escontrias decided that the building was too dangerous to hold classes until repairs were made. As a result, there was no school that year.

In answer to the district's problems, Socorro trustee and Texas Ranger, Silverio Escontrias, donated land at U.S. Highway 80 and Buford Road to the district for a school site. He donated three acres of land and sold the district

---

[2] The following information is reprinted with permission of the Socorro Independent School District. This information was found in a pamphlet entitled "The History of the Socorro Independent School District 1680-1984 by Kathleen Antwine and Jesus Fuentes.

four more acres at one-third the price. The original deed of August *24, 1921 states:*

"This is a deed of gift for the benefit of the School District aforesaid, and it is given with the distinct understanding that should said land cease to be used for school purposes in said district, that the title thereof shall revert to us and our heirs."

According to an El Paso Herald Post newspaper article dated June 28, 1921, the voters voted 32 to 1 to pass a twenty thousand dollar bond election to build the school. According to the article, doing away with the district entirely had been considered, with part of the pupils being sent to the Ysleta School and part to Clint, but this was not acceptable to the Socorro people as evidenced by their votes.

The school consisted of four big classrooms, two offices, cloak rooms, and a teacherage. The teacherage was a building to house single female teachers and consisted of five bedrooms, a kitchen, and a living room. It was the only teacherage in the county and was used until 1937.

Escontrias Elementary School opened in 1924 and was one of the largest schools in the county. It was located in the middle of cotton fields. In addition to the main building and teacherage, there was a baseball diamond, basketball courts, a track and field facility, gardens and a park. The tax rate was 29-1/8 cents per $100 evaluation for the maintenance of the school.

The adobe building was long and narrow, with a big pot belly stove in the center of the room. Every day the teacher, Miss Busque, would make a pot of hot soup for the children to eat for lunch. In 1924, students learned about carpentry, cotton farming, and raising animals through the vocational program.

Voters approved a $23,000 bond election in the summer of 1924 to fund the construction of four classrooms, an auditorium and a principal's cottage at Escontrias Elementary School. By 1926, the district enrollment had reached 452 students.

In the early 1930's, the County School Superintendent's Office began referring to Escontrias Elementary School as Socorro School in all newspaper articles and other correspondence. As a result, the school was called Socorro School from then on.

In the spring of 1981, the Board of trustees voted to change the name of Socorro Intermediate School to the building's original name of Escontrias Elementary School. On the Escontrias Elementary School's web-site, they have written:

"Escontrias Elementary would like to dedicate this web page to the Escontrias Family, and thank them for

their contributions.   It is because of their generosity and foresight, that we stand on this ground today, teaching generations of this community's children."

SOCORRO

DISTRICT NO. W-5

Trustees: Chairman, John O'Shea; Secretary, Silverio Escontrias; Mrs. William Moon.

AN attempt was made in 1921 to divide the Socorro district between Ysleta and Clint. This did not meet with the approval of the tax payers, and through the efforts of Silverio Escontrias who donated three acres of land, and sold four acres at one-third price for a school site, a $20,000 bond made possible the present school, consisting of four big class rooms, two offices, cloak rooms and a modern teacherage.

A new bond of $25,000 will be used this summer for the addition of four class rooms and an auditorium.

Many trees have been planted, 200 of which are growing; rose bushes, Shasta daisies and crysanthemums have been planted in the semicircle where the flag pole stands.

The 7th grade graduates for this year are: Alvina Ahrens, Dorothy Brice, Arcadia Chavez and James Escontrias.

This is the first year that any high school work has been given. The pupils in First Year High are shown in the picture on opposite page. They are, Evelyn Marler, Alva Collier, Anna Bovee, Wm. Marler, Irene Fortenberry, Cleo Cate. Top row, Hope Gordon, Thelma Cate, Alvina Ahrens and Mrs. Barnett, Principal. Winners of four blue, and four red ribbons in the County Day contest.

Also Home Economics and Vocational Agriculture were introduced this year. From the standpoint of the trustees, the patrons, and the pupils, the work has been very successful. The girls who have had a course in Domestic Art are as follows: bottom row, Evelyn Marler, Dera Cate, Irene Fortenberry, Dorothy Brice, Anna Bovee, Albina Ahrens, Myrtle Woods and Thelma Cate. Top row, Juana Dominguez, Arcadia Chavez, Consuelo Lujan, Helen Ahrens, Juanita Pruitt, Mary Brown, Hope Gordon, Lillian Pruitt and instructor, Miss Grayce Meadows. The boys who have had a course in vocational Agriculture are as follows: Left to right, Alva Collier, Cleo Cate, Wm. Marler, Louis Apodaca. Top row, Floyd Fortenberry, Isom Gordon, Oliver Collier, Jack Flynt, Nicholas Apodaca and Tobias Lujan. This class won first prize for welding.

Page Forty Two

Figure 67: Notes from a Socorro Board of Trustees Meeting

My family has attended two ceremonies. The first ceremony involved the official name change to Escontrias Elementary School on November 12, 1981 and members of the Silverio Escontrias family were honored guests. The second ceremony was held on October 27, 2004 at Escontrias Elementary School. The administrators, teachers, and children honored my father, Carlos Escontrias, with a beautiful program the year before he died.

Excerpt from a speech I gave to students at their Escontrias Elementary graduation:

…..My grandfather was a believer in education. Instead of cultivating crops on the land he donated, he cultivated minds. He wanted to have a school available for all children here in the lower valley.

A good education is what will open the door to your future. Don't ever let anything stop you! My message to you is to get good grades, respect your teachers and parents---have a goal, a dream in life.

And someday your dreams will come true!!

GOGGIN, HUNTER & BROWN
ATTORNEYS AT LAW
EL PASO, TEXAS

THE STATE OF TEXAS,)
COUNTY OF EL PASO.)

                KNOW ALL MEN BY THESE PRESENTS: That,

Silverio Escontrias, joined by his wife _Pilar_
Escontrias, of the County of El Paso, State of Texas, for and
in consideration of the sum of ONE DOLLAR to us paid by
E. B. McClintock, County Judge of El Paso County, Texas, have
GIVEN, GRANTED AND CONVEYED and by these presents do GIVE,
GRANT AND CONVEY to the said E. B. McClintock, County Judge of
El Paso County, Texas, and his successors in office for the
benefit of the School District of the Town of Socorro, in
El Paso County, Texas, that certain tract or parcel of land
situate, lying and being in the Socorro Grant, in El Paso
County, Texas, more particularly described as follows, to-wit:

        Beginning at the N.W. corner of the Escontrias
8.48 acre tract and the S.W. corner of the Andres
Chaves land and on the easterly side of the Socorro-
Belin road;
        Thence N. 54°10' E. and along the Southerly line
of the Andres Chaves tract 561.8 ft. to the westerly
line of the Franklin Canal;
        Thence S. 36°51' E. and along the Westerly line
of the Franklin Canal 252.3 ft.;
        Thence S. 54°10' W. 474.9 ft. to the easterly
line of the Socorro-Belen road;
        Thence N. 55°45' W. and along the easterly line of
the Socorro-Belen road 268.2 ft. to the place of beginning, containing three (3) acres of land.

      TO HAVE AND TO HOLD the said premises, together with
all and singular the rights, privileges and appurtenances
thereto in any manner belonging unto the said E. B. McClintock,
County Judge of El Paso County, Texas, and his successors in
office for the benefit of said school district, forever.

      This is a deed of gift for the benefit of the School
District aforesaid, and it is given with the distinct understanding that should said land cease to be used for school
purposes in said district, that the title thereof shall revert
to us and our heirs.
WITNESS OUR HANDS at El Paso, Texas, this __ day of August, 1921.

                        Silverio Escontrias

                        Pilar X Escontrias

Figure 68: Deed of gift for the benefit of the School District

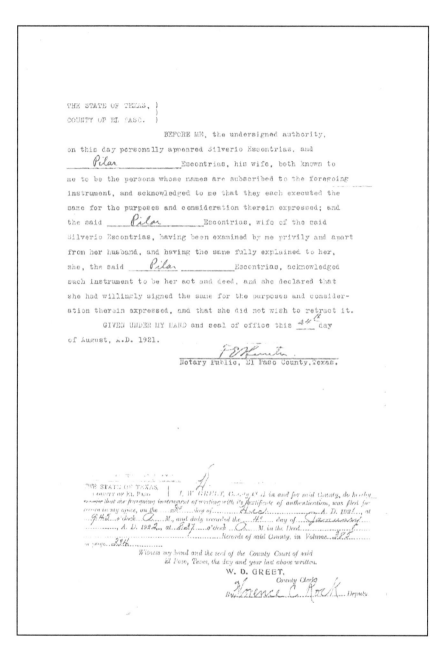

THE STATE OF TEXAS,)
COUNTY OF EL PASO.)

        BEFORE ME, the undersigned authority,
on this day personally appeared Silverio Escontrias, and
_____Pilar_____Escontrias, his wife, both known to
me to be the persons whose names are subscribed to the foregoing
instrument, and acknowledged to me that they each executed the
same for the purposes and consideration therein expressed; and
the said _____Pilar_____Escontrias, wife of the said
Silverio Escontrias, having been examined by me privily and apart
from her husband, and having the same fully explained to her,
she, the said ____Pilar____Escontrias, acknowledged
such instrument to be her act and deed, and she declared that
she had willingly signed the same for the purposes and consideration therein expressed, and that she did not wish to retract it.
        GIVEN UNDER MY HAND and seal of office this 24th day
of August, A.D. 1921.

                       Notary Public, El Paso County, Texas.

Figure 69: Page 2 of the Deed of Gift for the benefit of the School District

**Figure 70: Faculty and students at the Socorro School renamed
Escontrias Elementary School**

Figure 33: Believed to be the first class at the school built in Socorro, Texas

Figure 34: Escontrias Elementary School

Our school was named after Silverio Escontrias, an outstanding citizen in our area in the early nineteen hundreds. He acquired various land investments throughout his lifetime. Along with Juan Armendariz, Mr. Escontrias purchased the land now known as Hueco Tanks. Before long, a thriving cattle ranch, spanning six thousand acres, was established there. Later he acquired a tract of land on the outskirts of Ysleta, which produced cotton and alfalfa crops. Active management of the ranch was later turned over to his eldest son, while Mr. Escontrias oversaw the production of crops on the homestead farm.

Along with working to establish his family, Silverio Escontrias also demonstrated great interest in his community. In his younger days, he served as a member of the Texas Rangers which helped to establish law and order to this region of the "Wild West." Throughout his lifetime, he contributed to various charities and other worthy causes. In 1921, Silverio and his wife, Pilar, donated the land to the County of El Paso so that our school could be built.

Eleven years after his donation, Silverio Escontrias passed away at his home on the sixteenth of September. He was the father of eleven children: Juan, Manuela, Filberta, Fredencia, Jose, Pedro, Ramon, Santiago, Silverio Ramon II, and Carlos Escontrias.

Escontrias Elementary would like to dedicate this web page to the Escontrias Family and thank them for their contribution. It is because of their generosity and foresight, that we stand on this ground today, teaching generations of our community's children. From this donated land, a school has been established, winning a National Blue Ribbon Award and a Bronze Medal from National Center for Urban School Transformation in 2014, that daily instills our goal, "We Will All Succeed!"

Last Modified on August 5, 2014

Figure 35: Escontrias Elementary School Information on their website on 11/11/14

Figure 36: Believed to be the building phase of the Escontrias School

Come join us in thanking the
Escontrias family for their
generosity.

Their donation has polished
many shining stars.

Figure 37: Invitation for Escontrias Elementary School celebration

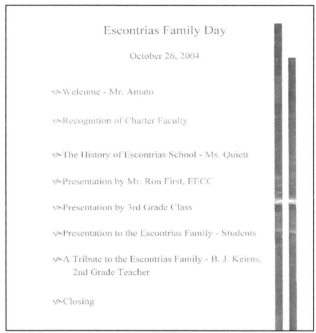

Figure 38: Invitation for Escontrias Family day

Figure 39: Carlos and Mary Escontrias and Beatrice Morales at the dedication ceremony to rename Socorro Elementary to Escontrias Elementary held on November 12, 1981

**Figure 40: Carlos Escontrias at a special ceremony held at
Escontrias Elementary School in his honor**

Figure 41: Ray Rodriguez, SISD former Board Member, and Roberto Duron, SISD former Superintendent, with Carlos Escontrias at a special ceremony at Escontrias Elementary School held in his honor.

Figure 42: Carlos Escontrias and Irma Escontrias Sanchez, Jaime Sanchez, Adrian Castaneda, Chris Castaneda, Ray Rodriguez, SISD former Board Member, and Roberto Duron, SISD former superintendent, at the ceremony held at Escontrias Elementary School

Figure 43: Adrian Castaneda, Chris Castaneda, Beatrice Morales, Denisa Morales, Peter Morales, Mary Alice Tellez, Irma Escontrias Sanchez, Patricia Castaneda, Jessica Macias and Carlos Escontrias at the ceremony held at Escontrias Elementary School

Figure 44: Irma Escontrias Sanchez, Peter Morales and Carlos Escontrias at the ceremony held at Escontrias Elementary School

Figure 45: Jessica Macias and Carlos Escontrias at the ceremony held at Escontrias Elementary School

Figure 46: Jessica Macias, Patricia Castaneda and Carlos Escontrias at the ceremony held at Escontrias Elementary School

Figure 47: Adrian Castaneda, Chris Castaneda, Irma Escontrias Sanchez, Beatrice Morales, Peter Morales, Mary Alice Tellez, Patricia Castaneda and Carlos Escontrias at the ceremony held at Escontrias Elementary School

Figure 48: Chris Castaneda, Jessica Macias, Patricia Castaneda, Albert Macias, Joseph Macias, Adrian Castaneda, Sandra Castaneda, and Carlos Escontrias at the ceremony held at Escontrias Elementary School

Figure 49: Denisa Morales, Adrian Castaneda, Chris Castaneda, Joseph Macias, Jessica Macias, Albert Macias, Michelle Morales and Peter Morales, with Carlos Escontrias at the special ceremony held at Escontrias Elementary School

Figure 50: Irma Escontrias Sanchez, Beatrice Morales, Mary Alice Tellez, and Patricia Castaneda with Carlos Escontrias at the special ceremony at Escontrias Elementary School

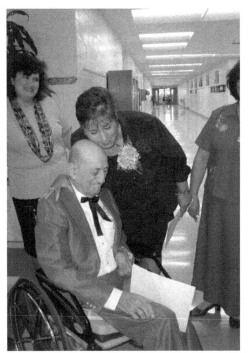

Figure 51: Irma Escontrias Sanchez, Patricia Castaneda, Mary Alice Tellez in background with Carlos Escontrias at the special ceremony held at Escontrias Elementary School

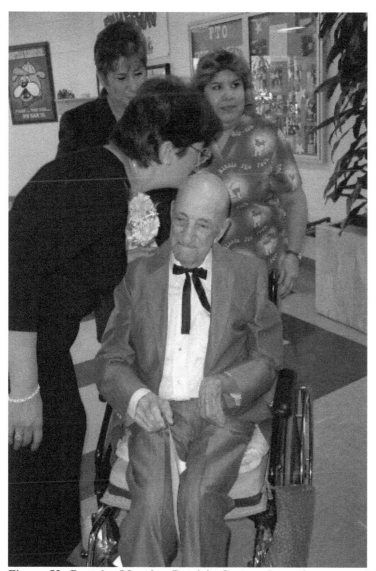

Figure 52: Beatrice Morales, Patricia Castaneda, and a nurse with Carlos Escontrias at the special ceremony at Escontrias Elementary School

Figure 53: Daughter, Mary Alice Tellez, Carlos Escontrias and a nurse at the special ceremony held at Escontrias Elementary School

Figure 54: Jaime and Irma Escontrias Sanchez with Carlos Escontrias at the special ceremony held at Escontrias Elementary School

**Figure 55: Escontrias Elementary School 25th Anniversary
Celebration**

**Figure 56: Escontrias Elementary School 25th Anniversary
Celebration**

**Figure 57: Escontrias Elementary School 25th Anniversary
Celebration**

Chapter 6
La Purisima Church/History of
Donated land

According to family oral history, my grandfather, Silverio Escontrias, donated seventeen acres of land to La Purisima Catholic Church in Socorro, Texas. I have not been able to find documentation to support this information, but I do know that growing up, my family attended La Purisima Catholic Church. My parents were life-long members of the congregation. To this day, there is a billboard standing next to my parent's home with information about La Purisima Catholic Church that has been there for years.

Figure 58: La Purisima Catholic Church in Socorro, Texas

Figure 59: La Purisima Catholic Church in Socorro, Texas as it stands today

Figure 60: San Jose Catholic Church in El Paso, Texas

Figure 61: San Jose Catholic Church in El Paso, Texas as it stands today

I did find documentation regarding the generosity of my grandfather regarding San Jose Catholic Church. An article in the El Paso Herald Post newspaper dated March 31st, 1972, cited a celebration of the seventy fifth anniversary of the San Jose Catholic Church. The article stated that Reverend Juan Cordova gave the first mass at the church and used to ride to the church on horseback to say Mass. Later, my grandfather, Silverio Escontrias, referred to as a well-to-do rancher from Socorro, gave Reverend Cordova a horse and buggy so that he could use that mode of transportation to get to the church.

Chapter 7
My Memories of my Mom and Dad,
Carlos and Maria Escontrias

Figure 62: Carlos and Maria Escontrias

My Mom told me that she remembered seeing my Dad for the first time on a beautiful horse. Their love story began on that day.

My parents were engaged on August 13, 1946. My Dad had invited my Mom out to eat the next day. He told her to "get all prettied up." They stopped at the ranch to leave off some groceries before heading out to eat on Montana Street which was Carlsbad Highway 62 at the time. My Dad told my Mom, "Before we go, let's go to the Tanke de la Virgen (Tank of the Virgen). Honey, let's climb up to that rock over there."

He was holding my Mom's hand since she was all dressed up. My Mom said my Dad asked her to accept his engagement ring. He took my Mom's picture which we have a copy of in the Hueco Tanks Interpretive Center. They went to eat and got married civilly on October 26, 1947, and by the Catholic Church on November 11, 1948.

I remember my Mother talking about growing up and working hard throughout her childhood. My mother finished school through fifth grade, but I have yet to meet someone who was as smart as she was. She was determined to make sure her younger brothers would attend school. She would iron for other people in order to make money to help her family. She would use this money to buy clothes for her brothers and sister. Even after she married my father, she would still make sure her own mother and father had plenty of food to eat.

Just like his own father, my father, Carlos Escontrias, was also a gifted horseman. In an El Paso Herald Post article dated May 19, 1952, reported the results of a calf match which indicated that the Ysleta Rough Riders won the tournament. My father was listed on the team roster.

My parents and siblings were and are very important to me. I am the youngest of four daughters....by a time frame of ten, eleven and twelve years. I grew up feeling a tremendous sense of love from my Mom. She was thrilled to find out she was expecting another child. The doctor thought she was imagining the pregnancy. My sisters were in school and she was excited at the thought of a new baby. They had hoped for a boy, but, surprise, I was a girl. My Dad was a truck driver and was gone a lot. My Dad drove his truck for ten years and never had an accident. I remember the eighteen wheeler parked on the street and the excitement of climbing into the cab.

I remember when I was growing up, my sisters Mary Alice, Beatrice, and Patricia were in a different world due to our age difference. This is probably why I became a teacher. I used to have to occupy myself since my sisters were all in school. Living in the lower valley of El Paso meant that I did not have many experiences most kids take for granted.

Luckily, I was turned on to reading by my fourth grade teacher and I then used books to travel the world I could only imagine. I used my dolls as students in the imaginary classroom I was teaching.

Attaining a higher education became one of my dreams. Being the first in my family to go to college was a goal I am proud of having achieved. My parents were the two smartest people in the world. However, my Dad completed an eleventh grade education and my Mom a fifth grade education. Our parents would read the newspaper and kept us up on world events. Don't get me wrong, I remember a rich life. I remember a time when we would always have a new car in the driveway.

But then we had a life changing event. My Dad had a stroke at the young age of fifty-three years old. This event changed our financial status and we now relied on Social Security disability benefits as well as a small pension. I remember my parents selling piece by piece the land they had owned for years. I never thought twice about it then, but I now realize the sacrifices they made for our well-being. I now think about the sacrifices they must have made when I wanted to participate in school activities such as cheerleading, which was an expensive activity. My Mother had the ability to stretch a dollar and never made me feel like I couldn't do something I set my sights on.

My mother and I had one of those friendships one can only dream of. We spoke on the phone every day and talked and talked about everything and nothing. My Mother taught me the value of faith. She always looked for the rainbow in every rainstorm. Both of my parents had great faith in all the saints. They had a special place in their bedroom for an altar of saints and candles. I now have those special saints in a special place in my own home. I remember the rituals of prayers said before I would leave the house. This faith would prove to be a necessity in the years to come.

It is amazing what we will all do for a loved one. My Mother had a history of kidney stones and one simple decision led us down another path in life. My Mom decided to change their health insurance, and I think the change in doctors impacted her future health. After a simple operation to remove a tumor, my Mom's wound got infected. Imagine a hole the size of baseball that had to heal from within. My sisters and I had to learn how to change and dress the wound. The doctor said she did not need chemotherapy. But, my Mom never really recovered from that surgery. My mother did not feel well at all. However, the doctors could not find a diagnosis. During my mother's last hospital stay, they found their answer…..my Mother had pancreatic cancer, and it had spread. We were told there was no hope for treatment. At that moment, I felt true despair at the thought of losing my Mother, my best friend. I lifted myself up, and immediately called my boss and told him I would not be returning to work. And then I mustered inner strength and prepared for the future. I never told her that treatment was not an option, but rather asked her if she just wanted to go home or get treatment. She opted to go home. And I knew before I asked that this would be her choice.

I had the wonderful fortune of being able to take a leave of absence from work with the full support of my boss and my family. Now I was taking care of my Mother as she had taken care of me. Life does go full circle. We had the help of many angels in the form of hospice nurses and caregivers. I had three sisters to share in the care of our Mother as her health deteriorated. At the same time, we were trying to care for our father whose own health had been affected by a stroke. The stroke had left the left side of his body paralyzed and he eventually had to use a wheelchair.

My mother had been the caregiver for my father. She taught us the value of unconditional love. She took those wedding vows to heart. She took care of my father and always gave him dignity and love. These are the lessons one can never teach, but rather show by example. For over twenty years since my Dad's stroke, my Mom had been the healthy one, the strong one, and now the tables had turned. Now I had to be the healthy one, the strong one and help to take care of them both.

Both my mother and father bestowed upon me the honor of being the one in the family whom they would choose to take care of their last wishes. I think this happened in part because I was the last daughter who had lived at home and had spent a lot of time with them while I went to school. It is an honor now, but at that time, it seemed like a load I could not carry. My parents also had my sisters and our entire family helping them during this difficult time. I thought of the footprints poem and I realized that when our family thought we could not walk anymore, God carried all of us. And I also know God carried my Mother.

During this time, I still had my own family to care for, but this is where my husband stepped in and became Mom and Dad for our children while I helped to care for my parents. My daughter, Cassie was fourteen years old and my son, Jaime was twelve years old at the time. My family never made me feel like I had to choose between them and my parents, and for that, I will be forever grateful to my husband and children.

My Mother was a planner and she planned for everything. She paid for the cemetery where her and my father would be buried and chose the headstones for their graves at the cemetery. She chose her outfit for her burial and let me know what suit she wanted my Dad to wear for his burial once he passed away. She planned for their wishes in their will when I was fifteen years old. I was amazed at all the preparation my Mother had done on a limited income. She gave me the gift of knowledge of every wish she had. Imagine the inner strength it took to show me all of her financial paperwork knowing that she was losing the independence she had fought so long to have. Imagine walking with me through their enormous house telling me what she would like for everyone to have. Imagine sorting through jewelry and being told what to give to each family member once both she and my Dad were gone.

My mother exhibited incredible strength and now I had to do the same. These rituals killed me inside, and sometimes she would see my tears. Mainly, I would cry by myself or when I came home. Little did I know that all of this planning would serve as the gift to hold our family together once she was gone. I am sure my Mother knew this all along.

My children, Cassandra and Jaime still talk about the daily visits with my parents. We would stop at the store to buy whatever was needed. I would spend many days and nights with my Mom and Dad. We talked and talked and talked. And as we spoke, I realized that each of my parents were books of knowledge and these books would soon no longer be with us. I regret not taking more time to write down the stories of their lives. One promise my Mother asked of me and my three sisters was to always love each other. She wanted our family to stay together once she was gone. The biggest promise my Mother asked me to make was to take care of my father once she was gone and I promised her that I would. We prepared for all of this with a power of attorney.

How sad it is to have someone come to the house to witness their signatures on documents that signify the ending of independence. But, my Mother wanted no stone unturned. She wanted to know that I would legally be able to care for my father once she was gone. Before she died, my Mom had already decided what suit my Dad would wear someday. Finally, my Mother asked me if everything was ready. I told her everything was ready, but I wasn't and knew I never would be. And in looking back, I realize my sisters were even less ready than I was. One of the toughest decisions my parents had agreed upon was to sign a living will which would ensure they would not be hooked up to life support. I made sure these wishes were followed. I did all that was asked of me and that is all any of us can do. Two months after we left the hospital, my Mother passed away. My sisters still can't believe the planning my Mom did in order for us to find peace in her passing

Again, this was part of my life's lessons. I now believe that sometimes our loved ones have to get so sick that you now ask God to take them and relieve their suffering. My mother died calling out to her own Mother. The hospice nurses told us that my Mother could see her own Mother at that point and was trying to reach her. This gesture cemented for me that I too will see my own Mother again and I wonder if I too will be calling for her when my time comes.

We were all so worried that we would have two funerals to plan because losing my Mother would be too much for my Father to bear. But, I think my father knew we could not bear another loss and found the strength to go through one year of life without my Mother. My father taught us true courage.

The year after my mother died was a year filled with making sure my father was able to live in his home….arranging for twenty-four hour care….coordinating schedules….paying bills….buying groceries….scheduling doctor visits and all without the guidance I so needed from my Mother. But it was also a year of spending the weekends watching movies with him, eating sweet bread from his favorite bakery, ordering his favorite tacos and just spending time together. I remember all the times my father would thank me. But, he was the one I needed to thank…..for having the courage to live one year without the woman he had loved for fifty six years.

My nephew, Peter, got married on a Saturday, and my father waited for us to get home to call us and tell us he was not feeling well. An ambulance was called and I rode in the ambulance. As we were racing to the hospital, I was asking my Mother if she was coming to get my Father. That night, my sisters and I all took turns being in the emergency room with my father while the others stayed in the waiting room. The next day, Sunday, we were all in his hospital room.

I remember planning to take my father home on Monday, but little did we know his life was slowly ebbing away. We all spent the day in his room talking and snoozing since we had not slept. My father kept waking up and looking at us. We talked about the wedding and about everyone who was in town. We were all confident we would still have more time together. We truly had no idea time was running out. Suddenly, my father's blood pressure began to drop. As he was dying, I was telling him my Mother was waiting for him in heaven. And I am sure she was there to greet him with open arms.

At the funeral, I spoke about how I felt like an orphan. In the span of one year, I had become an orphan and missed both of my parents desperately. I would now have time to spare.....time I would gladly lose again. I told my sisters someday we would all have our time back and this proved to be true. I learned to not wish for your life to be normal if you are caring for a loved one. Normal translates to missing your loved one more than you thought possible once they are gone. I would give anything to still be doing everything for both of them and more.

I now see other families and can't help feeling envy. I see Moms with their daughters spending time together. I see families sharing holidays together. And, as generous as our friends and family have been to us, I know in my heart that life will never be the same. The loss of my parents left a void in my life. And I also know that having had the love of two parents and losing it is much better than never having tasted that life at all.

I wonder if my parents were taken so that they could live together in a world without cancer or wheelchairs. I wonder if my parents were taken so that my own children could see love by examples they will never forget. I wonder if my parents were taken to show me that life is too short and we should not take the time we have for granted.

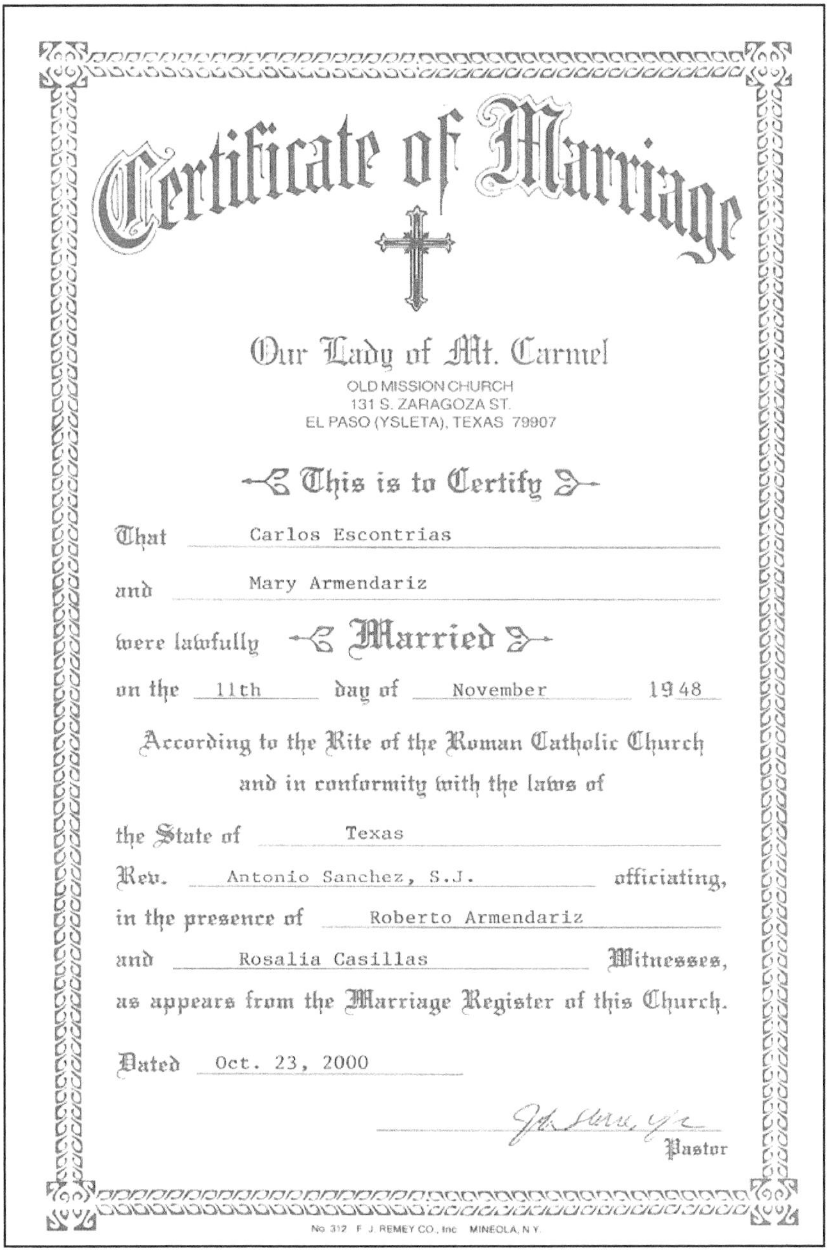

Certificate of Marriage

✝

Our Lady of Mt. Carmel

OLD MISSION CHURCH
131 S. ZARAGOZA ST.
EL PASO (YSLETA), TEXAS 79907

This is to Certify

That ___Carlos Escontrias___

and ___Mary Armendariz___

were lawfully **Married**

on the ___11th___ day of ___November___ ___1948___

According to the Rite of the Roman Catholic Church

and in conformity with the laws of

the State of ___Texas___

Rev. ___Antonio Sanchez, S.J.___ officiating,

in the presence of ___Roberto Armendariz___

and ___Rosalia Casillas___ Witnesses,

as appears from the Marriage Register of this Church.

Dated ___Oct. 23, 2000___

_____
Pastor

No. 312 F. J. REMEY CO., Inc. MINEOLA, N.Y.

Figure 63: Certificate of Marriage for Carlos Escontrias and Mary Armendariz

Figure 64: Carlos and Mary Escontrias

Figure 65: Carlos and Mary Escontrias

Figure 66: Carlos and Mary Escontrias

Figure 67: Carlos and Mary Escontrias

Figure 106: Carlos and Mary Escontrias

Figure 107: Carlos and Mary Escontrias

Figure 108: Carlos and Mary Escontrias

Figure 109: Carlos and Mary Escontrias

Figure 110: Carlos and Mary Escontrias

Figure 111: Carlos and Mary Escontrias

Figure 112: Carlos and Mary Escontrias

Figure 113: Carlos and Mary Escontrias

Figure 114: Carlos and Maria Escontrias

Figure 115: Carlos and Maria Escontrias

Figure 116: Carlos and Maria Escontrias

Figure 68: Carlos and Maria Escontrias

Figure 118: Carlos and Maria Escontrias

Figure 119: Slide from power point designed by Denisa Morales

Chapter 8
Carlos Escontrias

Figure 69: Carlos Escontrias and his horse Cinco

Eulogy I gave at my father's funeral

My Dad surprised us all by waiting almost exactly a year to join our Mother. And I think he did that because we couldn't bear another loss. We had all worried we would be burying them together when my Mom died.

But then again, our Dad was a miracle of his own. In ten years of driving big rigs, he had never had an accident. Even when he suffered a stroke in Amarillo, hundreds of miles away from home, he managed to drive his truck back home safely before getting to the hospital.

For twenty-six years he hung on to a changed life, realizing he could no longer work, walking with a cane, then a walker, and then finally a wheelchair. Many lesser humans would have given up long ago.

My Dad came from a rich history. His Dad, Silverio, was a Texas Ranger who donated land for the first school in Socorro. Land donations were also made to the Catholic Church.

My Dad lived a life of a true cowboy living both on the farm in Socorro as well as the ranch at Hueco Tanks. My Dad would go to school in Socorro and then spend one or two months working at the ranch in the summer. My Dad finished eleventh grade, but I think our family would tell you he was the smartest person we knew. He would read the newspaper from cover to cover and then proceed to tell each of us what was happening in the world.

"Barrozo" was my Dad's horse for 27 years. Barrozo was born at Hueco Tanks. When the foal was born, my Grandmother instructed the family to put the SE

Bar on it since that colt would be my Dad's horse. My Dad had that beautiful white gray horse for twenty-eight years and the horse was trained to rope, calf rope, and was an all-around great horse. My cousin, Yolanda was the barrel racer in the family, and she and my Dad would sit and talk about their adventures.

When it quickly became evident that our Dad was dying, the nurse told us to say goodbye and encourage him to go. I asked him if he could see my Mom standing there with his horse waiting to run off into the sunset. I told him he would be able to run once again into my Mother's waiting arms. And trust me; my Mom was waiting for him. We tried our best the year he lived after my Mom's death, but we weren't, and never could be, my Mom.

My Mom and Dad were married for fifty-six years. During that time, they were the heart of our family. The heartbeat was weaker the last year of my Dad's life without my Mom, and now both of their heartbeats are gone. Hopefully, we can go on in life with a different heartbeat.

We all are left with regrets of how we could all have done more the last year of my Dad's life. But, we are proud that my Dad was able to stay in his home his last year of life, still calling all the shots. None of us could have managed that feat alone. Everyone played a part in making sure that my Dad was taken care of. My sisters, Mary Alice, alias "Mickey Mouse", Bea and Patty,"las vecinas (the neighbors)", and me, "Little Gal" and then "Houston" , all stepped in to try to take the irreplaceable place of my Mom. We couldn't have done it without the help and support of Ruben, "el Colorado(Red)", Eloy, "el vecino (the neighbor)", George, "el arabe (the Arab)", and Jaime, "el abogado (the lawyer)".

All of the grandkids also would call or stop by bearing special treats for my Dad. Even my Dad's timing was right on the mark. He had been seeing visions of my Mom the past month before he died and I had told my sisters that I thought Mom would be coming for him soon. But she waited to take him until the day after my nephew's wedding. This was so like them both, thinking of everyone else and not themselves.

Regardless of the health problems my Dad faced, he never met a stranger, only friends. He treated each medical treatment with incredible grace and dignity. We could not have kept him home the last year of his life without the help of the wonderful people who helped us every step of the way. Dr. Luz Candelaria gave us support and guidance. Su Casa provided us with Marlene and Raul who helped guide us and care for him. A special program through VNA

(Visiting Nurse Association) brought us Carmen and Helen under the direction of Alby who helped to take care of my Dad every morning Monday through Friday. And Karen, from MHMR, who took on the role of counselor and supporter after my Mom died.

And last, but not least, our caretakers, Aracely and Freddy who made it possible for my father to live in his house and have round the clock care. To be perfectly truthful, they are the reason my Dad hung on. As long as he could live in his own house and remain the chief, he could deal with anything life sent him. Each person who visited and called touched my Dad by not forgetting him.

Without minimizing everyone else, I would like to especially thank the ones who never faltered and always visited my Dad and kept his spirits up- my Uncle Paul and Aunt Mary. Even through their difficult year filled with loss, they never failed to visit or call and see how my Dad was doing. Uncle Paul, my Mom knows all you did and will thank you someday.

I have thought a lot about legacies.....and what each person leaves behind once they pass. My grandfather truly left behind a lifetime of education for students attending the first school in Socorro. But legacies can be so much more....they don't have to be tied to money. My mother was a prime example of someone who will live forever in those she touched and loved. My Dad will leave behind a legacy of incredible strength mixed with humor. When my Mom was still alive, my Dad was in the hospital and made the huge mistake of referring to us daughters as "las trocas (trucks)". And I told him not to forget he was going home and would have to deal with the trocas (trucks). Now the trocas (trucks) will have to find a way to drive down that road of life without them.

My sisters and I will now be motherless and fatherless. We will look at other whole families with sadness and longing. But we wouldn't trade our parents for the world and we are grateful for the time God gave them to us. We pray to God to give us the strength to go on without them, and somehow, try to revive that heartbeat once again[3].

---

[3] From the Eulogy given by Irma Escontrias Sanchez

ESCONTRIAS

Carlos Escontrias Obituary

Carlos Escontrias, 79, made the journey from this life surrounded by his loving family on January 16, 2005. Carlos was a member of the Catholic Church and his rich family history included donations of land for Escontrias Elementary School as well as La Purisima Catholic Church. Carlos and his dearly departed wife, Maria, lived in Socorro. Their early years were spent at their former ranch which is now known as Hueco Tanks Historical State Park. Carlos was an extraordinary son, brother, husband, Dad, father-in-law, grandfather, and friend to all who knew him. Carlos never met a stranger, and made friends with everyone who came in contact with him. Carlos will be missed for his tremendous love, his incredible wisdom, his unending humor, and most of all for his strong family ethic.

Carlos is preceded in death by his loving wife of fifty-six years, Maria Escontrias, his parents, Silverio and Pilar Escontrias, his brothers, Juan, Jose, Pedro, Ramon, Santiago, Silverio, Ramon II, and his sisters, Manuela, Filberta, and Fredencia.

Carlos is survived by his daughters, Mary Alice Tellez, Beatrice Morales, Patricia Castaneda, and Irma Escontrias Sanchez. Carlos was the last remaining son of Silverio and Pilar Escontrias. Our family would like to thank all who called and supported him after our Mother's passing earlier this year. A very special thank you goes out to Paul and Mary Armendariz who became our family's guardian angels this year. Honorary pallbearers include his brothers-in law Pete and Paul Armendariz along with his loving sons-in-laws, Ruben Tellez, Eloy Morales, George Castaneda, and Jaime Sanchez. The pallbearers will be his devoted grandchildren Ruben and Ralph Tellez, Ernie and Peter Morales, and Gabriel and Chris Castaneda. Additional grandchildren include Denisa Morales, Jessica Macias, Adrian Castaneda, and Cassandra and Jaime Sanchez. Carlos's additional great-grandchildren include Julian and Josiah Tellez, Mel and Gabriel Castaneda, and Nathan and Joseph Macias. His extended grandchildren by marriage include Melissa Tellez, Sandra Castaneda,

Albert Macias and Michelle Morales who never waivered in their love and support during this time. A very special thanks goes out to Father Vincent of Mt. Carmel Parish and Father Juan of La Purisima parish. We would also like to thank Dr. Candelaria and Dr. Hayes, along with the staff of Su Casa to include Marlene and Raul who provided my father with his home healthcare support. We also appreciate the daily support the VNA staff provided which included Alby, Carmen and Helen as well as the support provided by Karen of the MHMR services. We would especially like to thank Aracely and Freddy for their daily care of our father. We also appreciate the support Socorro ISD and Ysleta ISD (Desert View Middle School) extended to our entire family during this past year. Visitation will be on Tuesday, January 18th from 2p.m. to 5 p.m. at Hillcrest Funeral Home-Carolina. Vigil Service will be Tuesday, January 18th at 7 p.m. at Our Lady of Mount Carmel Catholic Church. Funeral Mass will be Wednesday, January 19th at 10a.m. at Our Lady of Mount Carmel Catholic Church. Interment will be at Evergreen East Cemetery. Directed by HILLCREST FUNERAL HOME. 1060 CAROLINA DR. 598-3332.

H.R. No. 444

RESOLUTION

WHEREAS, The certain knowledge of a life well lived tempers the profound sadness the passing of Carlos Escontrias on January 16, 2005, at the age of 79, brings to all who knew and loved this esteemed Socorro resident; and

WHEREAS, Mr. Escontrias valued the importance of education and held dear his strong faith, and he took justifiable pride in his family's donation of the lands on which Escontrias Elementary School and La Purisima Catholic Church were built; and

WHEREAS, This devoted family man enjoyed an enduring relationship with his wife of 56 years, Maria, and the early years of their marriage were spent at their former ranch, known today as Hueco Tanks State Historical Park; during their union, Mr. and Mrs. Escontrias were blessed with four daughters and many grandchildren and great-grandchildren; and

WHEREAS, Widely admired for his wisdom, humor, and devotion to friends and family, Carlos Escontrias will be greatly missed, but his spirit will live on in the hearts of the many people whose lives he touched; now, therefore, be it

RESOLVED, That the House of Representatives of the 79th Texas Legislature hereby pay tribute to the life of Carlos Escontrias and extend deepest sympathy to the members of his family: to his daughters, Mary Alice Tellez and her husband, Ruben, Beatrice Morales and her husband, Eloy, Patricia Castaneda and her husband, George, and Irma Sanchez and her husband, Jaime; to his grandchildren, Ruben and Ralph Tellez, Ernie and Peter Morales, Gabriel, Chris, and Adrian Castaneda, Denisa Herrera, Jessica Macias, and Cassandra and Jaime Sanchez; to his great-grandchildren, Julian and Josiah Tellez, Mel and Gabriel Castaneda, and Nathan and Joseph Macias; to his extended grandchildren by marriage, Melissa Tellez, Sandra Castaneda, Albert Macias, Bobby Herrera, and Michelle Morales; and to his other relatives and many friends; and, be it further

RESOLVED, That an official copy of this resolution be prepared for the members of his family and that when the Texas House of Representatives adjourns this day, it do so in memory of Carlos Escontrias.

Quintanilla

Figure 70: Resolution certified that H.R. No. 444 was unanimously adopted by a rising vote of the House on March 3, 2005

Figure 71: Carlos Escontrias and his horse "Cinco"

**Figure 72: Barrozo, the horse that Pilar Escontrias gave to her son,
Carlos Escontrias**

Figure 73: Carlos Escontrias competing at the Rough Riders in El Paso, TX

Figure 74: Carlos Escontrias

Figure 75: Carlos Escontrias and Robert Armendariz

Figure 76: Carlos Escontrias and the Casillas'

Figure 77: Carlos Escontrias at the Tanque de la Virgen

Figure 78: Carlos Escontrias rock climbing

Figure 79: Carlos Escontrias

Figure 131: Carlos Escontrias

Figure 132: Carlos Escontrias and Paul Armendariz

Figure 133: Carlos Escontrias

Figure 134: Carlos Escontrias

Figure 135: Carlos Escontrias

Chapter 9
Maria Escontrias

Figure 136: Maria Escontrias

Eulogy I gave at my mother's funeral

On behalf of our family, we would like to thank each and every one of you who have loved our Mother and helped hold her hand while she made her journey to heaven.

My Mom was an extraordinary woman who was always taking care of others throughout her life. My grandmother, Margarita Armendariz, became ill and my Mom stepped in at the age of eight years old to become a little mother to her brothers and sisters. She would make food, iron their clothes, bathe them and provide all the love she could at that young age. She worked cleaning houses and ironing clothes and one of her goals was for my Uncle Charlie to always look nice for school. This is the reason my Uncle Charlie and Uncle Paul always said she was their second mother. We all learned by example how to take care of my Mother because my sisters saw my Mom do the same for her own Mother.

Once my Mom married my Dad, she helped care for my Grandmother Pilar throughout her battle with diabetes. My Dad was a truck driver and for ten years my Mom would be Mom and Dad to all of us. My Mom remained a tough little woman….and we remember her going out with a gun when she would hear the cows making noise outside. She was fearless. My Mom and my Tia (Aunt) Chavela even shot a snake at the former family ranch now known as Hueco Tanks. The only problem was that the snake hadn't died when they put it in the trunk of the car. When my Dad had his stroke when I was sixteen years old, my Mom stood by him and took care of him until the very end. She never complained and never failed him throughout their fifty six years of marriage.

Growing up, our family has so many memories all about my Mom. Everyone come eat at my Mom's house and the food would magically multiply. She was the most generous person I will ever know. We had great holidays together: Easter at Hueco Tanks, Fourth of July at my Mom and Dad's house, and boy, was Christmas a joyous time for my Mom. We spent a day together wrapping everyone's Christmas gifts before she died….still thinking of everyone even while she was dying.

When we first learned of the extent of her illness, many family members wanted to know when they should come, and I told them to come see her and talk to her while she was alive….when it really counts. And boy, did you come! Many of our family members flew in or drove all night to be with her. And we talked!!! You could pass by her room at any given time and she would be surrounded by her daughters, her brothers, sisters, sisters-in-law, godchildren, grandchildren, great-grandchildren and friends who loved her like their own Mother. I wish we could have had a video recorder recording the special conversations….but, we all have those special conversations recorded in our hearts where they will remain forever. My Mom would ask why God was waiting so long to take her, and I told her it was for all of us...so that we could have time to say goodbye to her.

My Mother was "surrounded by love"....I think this would be my Mom's happiest legacy. She was never, for one minute, left alone.....thanks to our family and friends and the love her daughters had for her. It is amazing and comforting to know how everyone in our lives have stepped in and offered gestures that will add up to the special memories we will hold dear in our hearts.

Did you call?

Did you send a card?

Did you send an item like a special gift, food, baked goods, paper goods, a special Pope John Paul medal, a handmade shawl, fruit, nuts or money for a Thanksgiving meal?

Or did you silently pray for her?

Anything you did was appreciated and helped us so much through this difficult time.

I would like to thank my sisters and all of our immediate family for never forgetting my Mother throughout this time. I read a book that explained that in each family each sibling has a role to play. Mary Alice was the "Doctor" who stayed calm and helped us know what to do. Bea was the "Housekeeper" who kept the house spotless. Patty was the "Cook" who was always cooking throughout each day. And they tell me I was the "Director"....now, isn't that interesting? All I know is that I am grateful to my sisters who stood hand in hand with me and helped make my Mom's days happy and peaceful ones.

Now, let me tell you about a brother who loved my Mom like his own Mother. My Uncle Paul couldn't do enough for my Mom. He would bring her food to try to tempt to open her appetite and built an altar for her Nativity set. When that was finished, he then made her a heart of lights at the entrance of her house to signify his love for her and the light she had been for him. We may have turned off the lights, but their special light will never dim.

One night, we gathered around my Mom and each of us told her what she meant to each of us.

"You light up my sad days."

"You teach the unteachable."

"You gave me unconditional love."

"You were a role model for us all."

"You were always there for us".

"You made me a better person."

And the words went on and on.

My Mom was a loving daughter, a superb and loyal wife, a fantastic Mother, grandmother and great grandmother, and a caring sister. She also managed to inspire love in all the people she met throughout her life.

Thank you to all of you who walked this journey with us....each of you helped her get to heaven through your prayers, calls, visits.....and loved her to the very end. Father Vincent, Dr. Luz Candelaria, and the staff of La Mariposa Hospice helped us with her spiritual and physical care.

I have no doubt she will live on in the memories no one can ever take from us-the strong legacy of a loving woman and Mother. In each positive characteristic we find in one another, we will know she planted it there....and she will remain alive in each of us.

ESCONTRIAS

Mary Escontrias Obituary

Maria A. Escontrias made the journey from this life surrounded by her loving family at home on January 12, 2004. Maria was a member of the Catholic Church and remained true to her faith during her illness. Carlos and Maria's primary residence remains in Socorro, and much of their early years were spent at their former ranch which is now known as Hueco Tanks Historical Park. Maria was an extraordinary daughter, sister, wife, mother, mother-in-law, grandmother, great-grandmother and friend to all who knew her. Maria will be missed for her tremendous love, her incredible wisdom, her unending humor, and most of all for her legacy of a strong family ethic. Maria is preceded in death by her parents, Francisco and Margarita

Armendariz and her brothers Robert and Carlos Armendariz. Maria is survived by her husband of fifty-six years, Carlos Escontrias, and daughters, Mary Alice Tellez, Beatrice Morales, Patricia Castaneda, and Irma Escontrias Sanchez. She is also survived by her dear brothers, Pete and Paul Armendariz and sister Maria Elena Acosta, who, along with their extended families, remained by her side through her journey of life and never faltered in their love and support through her illness. Inez Armendariz, Mary Armendariz and Socorro Armendariz remained by her side as well. Honorary pallbearers include her brothers Pete and Paul Armendariz along with her loving sons-in-laws, Ruben Tellez, Eloy Morales, George Castaneda and Jaime Sanchez. The pallbearers will be her devoted grandchildren, Ruben and Ralph Tellez, Ernie and Peter Morales, and Gabriel and Chris Castaneda. Additional grandchildren include Denisa Morales, Jessica Macias, Adrian Castaneda and Cassandra and Jaime Sanchez. Maria's additional great-grandchildren include Julian and Josiah Tellez, Mel and Gabriel Castaneda, and Nathan and Joseph Macias. Her extended grandchildren by marriage include Melissa Tellez, Sandra Castaneda and Albert Macias who never waivered in their love and support. Our family would like to thank all of our extended family and friends for their unfailing love and support during this time. A very special thanks goes out to Father Vincent of Mt. Carmel parish, Dr Luz Candelaria, and the staff of La Mariposa Hospice to include Claudia and Blanca who provided spriritual and physical care to our Mother. We also appreciate the support Socorro ISD and Ysleta ISD (Desert View Middle School) extended to the entire family. Visitation will be Wednesday, January 14, 2004 from 2p.m. to 5 p.m. at Hillcrest Funeral Home-Carolina. Vigil Service will be Wednesday at 7p.m. at Our Lady of Mount Carmel Catholic Church. Funeral mass will be Thursday at 10 a.m. at Our Lady of Mount Carmel Catholic Church. Internment will be in Evergreen East Cemetery. Directed by HILLCREST FUNERAL HOME. 1060 CAROLINA DR. 598-3332.

Mother's Day Speech I gave celebrating my Mother,

Maria Escontrias

I would like to wish all of you a wonderful Mother's Day. I am here to celebrate my own mother's legacy and although it is with sadness that I stand before you, it is also with great joy at having had the most wonderful mother anyone can ask for. You see, I lost my mother on January 12, 2004. And as painful as that was, I will always be grateful for having the wonderful mother I was given. I am here to tell you all that my mother, Mary Escontrias, taught me. We could be here all day, but I will try to keep my talk to a decent length.

*My mother taught me the true meaning of wedding vows.

'In sickness and in health"-you see my father had a stroke at the young age of 53 and my Mother cared for him until her last breath. She always gave him his place as the head of the household and never made him feel "less than" because of his disabilities. And even as she was dying from pancreatic cancer, she asked me to make sure I would take care of my father as well….and I made her that promise and kept my word.

My own husband has had some health challenges in the form of an optic nerve tumor and a malignant kidney tumor. And I have tried to rise to the level of love I saw in my own mother….trying to live my life by her example. I want my own children to see that those wedding vows are filled with meaning and that I have tried to live them myself. I am thankful that my husband has regained his health. We may have more challenges down the road, but I will be by his side as I know he will be by mine if I ever become ill.

"In richer or poorer"-when my father became disabled, our family income was affected although you would never know it. My mother knew how to stretch a dollar and never made me feel like I couldn't do anything even if it meant needing money. I was a cheerleader in high school and went to UTEP and she never made me feel like I couldn't do those things due to our financial means. As an adult, I wonder how she managed.

I too know the meaning of "in richer or poorer". Jaime was still in law school when we married and I moved to Houston. I was the sole support for two years. But this experience gave us the chance to grow in our marriage and appreciate all that we have....knowing that as long as we had each other, we would be fine.

*My mother taught me the true meaning of forgiveness

My Dad's parents were not supportive of my father marrying my mother. My parents even eloped to Las Cruces. Yet, my mother took care of my grandmother, Pilar Escontrias, until she passed away. My grandmother had diabetes and had both legs amputated and was in a wheelchair. But my mother showed us the true meaning of forgiveness in her actions.

She always talked to me about forgiveness and being there for those who might not treat you well, but she actually lived those words herself. I know that I too will do whatever is called on me to do for my family.

*My mother taught me the meaning of true intelligence and sacrifice

My mother only went to school through fifth grade. Yet, she was the smartest person I know. She used to iron and clean houses so that my uncles could have decent clothes and shoes for school. She would iron their clothes and basically sacrificed her own education for them. My uncles talk about my mother as their second mother.

One of my mother's proudest days was on the day I graduated from UTEP. I worked as a recreation leader, a music teacher and a waitress. I too worked hard to achieve being the first in my family to attain a college education. But, how could I not with my mother as a role model.

*My mother taught me how to honor your parents

My mother was there for my grandma and grandpa as well....her own parents. She would take my grandmother to buy groceries and would be there for them day and night. She taught me that bond of love between a mother and a daughter by example. My grandmother asked my Aunt Nena to take my mother out of her hospital room because my mother would not let her die. My own mother had to be hospitalized because of her own grief at the loss of her mother.

I too remember trying to be there for my own parents. I loved taking them on trips. When my mother became ill, the visits would be on a daily basis....and we would pick up groceries on the way to the house. We would spend weekends there and try to watch movies and buy their favorite foods. My own children have seen my example how to honor your parents and they still miss my parents....as I do every single day.

In retrospect, all I did for my own mother and father came from the example of my own mother.

*My mother taught me the importance of having good friends

The Golden Girls....that is what we called my mother and her special friends. The special friends who are there for each other in good times and in bad. The special friends you support through illness and loss of spouses. The special friends you travel with and go shopping with. The special friends you go to the Bingo with and call daily just to talk about anything and nothing. The special friends who would call my father when my mother died to check on him and see how he was doing.

I have been lucky to have special friends in my life. Those friends that have been there through the illnesses and loss of my parents.....through the two periods of illness of my husband......through the joyful celebrations that life also brings to us. They say that if you have one good friend in life, you are lucky....and I have been beyond lucky....as was my mother.

*My mother taught me the importance of faith

I remember going to church every Sunday. I remember my mother's special candles and her Virgen de Guadalupe along with all of her saints. I remember her deep devotion to San Lorenzo and her knowledge that if you prayed to a certain saint your prayer would be answered. I remember the special prayer she would say whenever one of us left the house.

Sombra de San Pedro/*Shadow of St. Peter*
"La sombra de San Pedro/*May the shadow of St. Peter*
Te bendizga cruz y cruz/*Bless you in the sign of the cross*
Que no te pase nada domas de mi dulce Jesus/*That nothing may happen to you, that my sweet Jesus*

Que te lleve con salud y felicidad/*Bless you with health and happiness*

Llevame y tragaime con bien"/*Take me and bring me safely*

Oración/Prayer

Santo Apóstol, Pedro Clemente,/Holy Apostle, Merciful Peter

De mi no apartes tu protección,/Do not leave me unprotected,

A ti me acojo yo reverente/In you I take reverant comfort

Y elevo humilde esta petición,/and I make this humble prayer

Cubreme, sombra del mas sublime/Cover me, shadow of the greatest

De los pastores, tenme piedad,/of the sheperds have mercy on me,

Aparta siempre de mi destino/always keep my destiny

Toda miseria y enfermedad./all misery and infirmity

Quien no me quiera que huya de mi,/May those who do not want me, stay away from me

Las personas adversas apartalas,/Keep me from my adversaries

Bendice, Pedro, tu mi camino/St. Peter, bless my journey

Y no me dejes nunca penar,/and never let me suffer

I too have tried to live a good Catholic life. If you marry someone who was going to be a priest, this is pretty much expected. I struggle with knowing that I am imperfect and am not on the level I see so many others are. But, I try to be worthy of the role models I have been lucky enough to have.

*My mother taught me the importance of loving your inner circle of family

I remember my mother gathering me and my sisters around her hospital bed and asking us to promise to always love each other. She knew her illness and leaving us to care for my father had posed challenges for us, and she wanted to know that we would always love each other once she was gone.

And I find myself repeating this with my own children. I tell them they will always have each other and to love one another. I wait for that day when they will become friends and support one another. Going through the loss of two parents in one year presented many challenges for me and my sisters. But, we are building those bonds once again with the knowledge that we only have each other to hold onto.

*My mother taught me the importance of loving your extended family

I remember gatherings at my Mom and Dad's home. I remember my mother feeding so many people and the pots never seeming to run out of food. I remember holiday gatherings and gatherings just meant to get together. I remember poker games with my aunts and uncles where I would hope to be able to play.

And now some of those gatherings are now taking place at my house. I remember planning special gatherings to celebrate special occasions. And in looking at our photo albums, it gives me great happiness to see my family celebrating our love at my home.

*My mother taught me the importance of planning

I remember my mother not wanting any of us to worry about funeral expenses when she or my father passed away. Somehow she managed to pre-pay the cemetery costs for both her and my father. She made sure that my sisters and I did not have to worry about these costs. She even told me what dress she wanted to wear and what suit she wanted for my father. She walked around the house with me indicating what she wanted each family member to have once they were both gone. This may sound difficult to do, and it was, but it was a great gift once they were gone and everyone knew their exact wishes. She entrusted me with the role of executor, gave me the power of attorney, and made sure I would be able to carry on with the care of my father.

And when my husband Jaime became ill, I was grateful we had also planned. We did not plan to the extent that my mother had, but at least we could concentrate on his getting well instead of thinking about living wills, wills, etc. I know his wishes and he knows mine and that is the greatest gift we can give each other as well as our children.

*My mother taught me the importance of generosity

In retrospect, I don't know how she did it, but giving gifts gave my mother great joy. She always made sure she had birthday gifts and Christmas gifts for everyone. Even for her last Christmas with us, she had me wrapping the gifts she had bought that year.

My friends tease me that I buy gifts and don't even know who will receive them. I inherited that giving spirit from my Mother. Even making someone a gift or copying a poem will brighten someone's day.

*My mother taught me the importance of setting limits

When we were growing up, my father was a truck driver and was gone a lot. So my mother was both the mother and father to us. She was very strict and I remember complaining that I had to always come home earlier that anybody else. But, as an adult, I was so grateful to her for setting those limits. She expected me and my sisters to live a good life which included expectations and consequences.

And now I struggle to do the same with my own children. I am lucky in that I can talk to them about my own limits that my mother set…and that we do it out of love for them. Sometimes those storms between a mother and her children are hard to weather, but I know there will be a rainbow someday.

*My mother taught me the importance of having fun

My mother was a gambler. She loved going to the casinos and I remember the fun she would have on trips we took to Las Vegas. She also loved Bingo. I remember how frustrated she would get when I would go with her to the

Bingo and be more concerned about going to the snack bar instead of taking care of my cards.

I enjoy these activities as well. No, I am not going to Gamblers Anonymous, but I think I enjoy the times my sisters and I do go to the casino because it reminds us of the fun she always had.

My mother taught me fashion

My mother was a stay at home Mom. But, she always looked like a million bucks. She always had on nice pant suits and had her hair fixed. I used to call her Liz Taylor.

She taught me to always have pride in your appearance. I don't get as dressed up as she used to, but I try to look presentable.

My mother taught me courage

We used to have cows and horses. And since my Dad was gone a lot, my mother would go outside whenever she would hear a noise. She was courageous and didn't hesitate to protect her family.

Well, she tried to teach me courage. She used to say she couldn't believe what chickens me and my sisters were. And she was right.

My mother taught me how to be crafty

My mother would paint ceramics and even had her own kiln. She would take pride in decorating her Christmas tree and would make beautiful floral arrangements. She would learn how to make flags out of safety pins and would paint tablecloths.

I am not very crafty, but I have self-taught myself to sew and to learn how to make angels. I even took a class on how to make stained glass. And I know I got that sense of trying to learn new things from my mother.

My mother taught me how to be a doctor

My mother would cure anything….and I do mean anything. She had remedies for migraines…..for stomach aches…..for cuts and scrapes. Some of our fondest memories are remembering my mother with tweezers ready to attack an earring holder that had gone into one of my nephew's ears. It is amazing how a mother can make anything feel better.

OK, I am not the doctor in my family. Jaime thinks he is the one who is the doctor. Don't ever tell him you don't feel well….because you will find yourself quickly getting medication as he self-diagnoses your ailment.

My mother taught me to be a hard worker

My mother took care of a huge house. If you ever came over, everything was spotless and in its place. But she never made her grandchildren feel like they couldn't play and make a mess. She would be right there making a mess with them telling us to let them play and be children. She was an excellent cook who could throw together a huge meal in a few minutes. I was always in awe of how she could reach into that magic refrigerator and pantry and find everything she needed.

Having her as a role model made me become a hard worker too. I like to take on extra projects and do the best job I can.

My mother taught me true lessons in life

My mother taught me how to love others and try to do so unconditionally.

My mother taught me to be loyal to others.

My mother taught me to appreciate everyone and never make anyone feel "less than".

My mother taught me that life is too short and you must embrace every moment you have since it may be the last.

So I am here to ask you to embrace your mother or that person in your life who has been like a mother to you. Be proud of the mother you have been. Are we perfect? No. We just try to do the best we can. Many of us face the challenge of taking care of our mothers while trying to juggle so many other roles. Please know that I would give anything to do it all again…. And I look forward to the day I see my mother once again and we talk about everything and nothing.

Figure 137: Maria Escontrias

Figure 138: Maria Escontrias and her brother Pete Armendariz

Figure 139: Maria Escontrias and Chavela Escontrias

Figure 140: Maria Escontrias   **Figure 141: Maria Escontrias and Irene Armendariz Subia**

Figure 142: Maria Escontrias and Chavela Escontrias

Figure 143: Maria Escontrias

Figure 144: Maria Escontrias with family members

Figure 145: Maria Escontrias   **Figure 146: Maria Escontrias**

Figure 147: Maria Escontrias

Figure 148: Maria Escontrias

Figure 149: Maria Escontrias

Chapter 10
Family Visits to Hueco Tanks

Figure 150: Carlos and Maria Escontrias, Irma Escontrias Sanchez, Yolanda Murphy, Patricia Castaneda, Mary Alice Tellez and Beatrice Morales

I realize that visiting Hueco Tanks was a difficult task for my father. This magical place was once his home. And now he and his family were visitors. But, Alex Mares and Wanda Olszewski, two of the park rangers, worked hard to build a relationship with my father and his family.

They made us feel welcome and special whenever we visited the park for a celebration. Our family is grateful for the time our parents and extended family have spent at the park reliving the past and honoring our family members.

Hueco Tanks will always hold memories, each priceless to the bearer. For my Mom, memories include living a life with a lot of family members....for my Dad, memories include living the life of a cowboy riding horses and chasing cattle. For my sisters and I, memories include Easter gatherings and all the fun of a picnic. We would be chasing after our cousins with the added problems of either keeping up or being left behind.

For visitors, Hueco Tanks brings the ability to enjoy rock climbing and looking at the pictographs. You are able to visit a state park filled with lots to do, see and enjoy.

Once we are all long gone, the beauty and wonder of Hueco Tanks will live on. And how fitting to know that generations to come will see this Escontrias home and wonder about the lives of the people who once lived there.

Again, I would like to thank Wanda for including the Escontrias family in the Hueco Tanks celebrations. A special thanks to all of the park staff who are committed to taking care of the park and insuring that my children and

my children's children will be able to enjoy all the park has
to offer in the years to come.

**Figure 151: Carlos and Maria Escontrias, Irma Escontrias
Sanchez, Mary Alice Tellez, Fred and Yolanda Murphy**

Figure 152: Wanda Olszewski and Carlos Escontrias

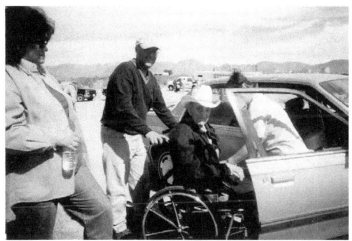

Figure 153: Carlos Escontrias and Jaime and Irma Escontrias Sanchez

Figure 154: Irma Escontrias Sanchez speaking at Hueco Tanks Interpretive Fair

Figure 155: Maria Escontrias and Wanda Olszewski

Figure 156: Carlos Escontrias, Mary Alice Tellez, Patricia Castaneda, Cassandra Sanchez, Maria Elena Acosta and family members

Figure 157: Paul Armendariz, Mary Armendariz and Maria Elena Acosta at Hueco Tanks

Figure 158: Beatrice Morales, Patricia Moncada, Mary Alice Tellez and Patricia Castaneda

Figure 159: Maria Escontrias reminiscing

Figure 160: Maria Escontrias pointing at Escontrias names

Figure 161: Maria Escontrias

Figure 162: Jessica Macias, Patricia Castaneda, Irma Escontrias Sanchez, Beatrice Morales, Denisa Morales and Maria Escontrias

Figure 163: Maria Escontrias, Irma Sanchez, Jaime Sanchez, Wanda Olszewski and Hueco Tanks staff members

Figure 164: Maria Escontrias with Evangeline Ramirez, Tony and Dahlia Gongora and Jaime and Irma Escontrias Sanchez

Figure 165: Maria Escontrias with Jessica Castaneda, Patricia Castaneda, Denisa Morales, Beatrice Morales and Irma Escontrias Sanchez

Figure 166: Maria Escontrias, Jessica Castaneda, Denisa Morales, Beatrice Morales, Patricia Castaneda and family members

Figure 167: Cassandra Sanchez with family members at Hueco Tanks

Figure 168: Carlos Escontrias, Maria Elena Acosta, Gabriel Castaneda, Mary Armendariz, Paul Armendariz, Jaime Sanchez and family members

**Figure 169: Jaime A. Sanchez, Cassandra Sanchez, Peter Morales
and Beatrice Morales picnicking at Hueco Tanks**

Figure 170: Gloria Lopez and Irma Escontrias Sanchez

Figure 171: Nathan Macias, Jaime Sanchez, Jessica Macias and Cassandra Sanchez

Figure 172: Jaime A. Sanchez, Erin Macias, Joseph Macias, Cassandra Sanchez and Nathan Macias

Figure 173: Gabriel Castaneda, Juni Castaneda, Melissa Castaneda, Sandra Castaneda, Peter Morales, Olivia Morales and Ernie Morales

Figure 174: Mary Armendariz, Mary Alice Tellez, Patricia Castaneda, Beatrice Morales and Irma Escontrias Sanchez

Figure 175: Mary Armendariz, Olivia Morales, Mary Alice Tellez, Patricia Castaneda, Beatrice Morales, Irma Escontrias Sanchez, Jaime Sanchez, Patricia Moncada and Carlos Moncada

Figure 176: Jaime and Irma Escontrias Sanchez

Figure 177: Irma Escontrias Sanchez, Beatrice Morales, Mary Alice Tellez and Patricia Castaneda

Figure 178: Patricia Castaneda, Beatrice Morales, Dahlia Gongora, Mary Alice Tellez and Irma Escontrias Sanchez

Figure 179: Cassandra Sanchez, Mary Alice Tellez, Jaime A. Sanchez, Patricia Castaneda, Irma Escontrias Sanchez, Beatrice Morales and Dahlia Gongora

Figure 180: Patricia Castaneda, Irma Escontrias Sanchez and Beatrice Morales

Figure 181: Back row: Gabriel Castaneda, Patricia Castaneda, Irma Escontrias Sanchez, Jaime Sanchez, Jessica Macias, Adrian Castaneda, Beatrice Morales   Front row: Nathan Macias, Sandra Castaneda, Juni Castaneda, Mary Armendariz and Paul Armendariz

Figure 182: Tribute to Silverio Escontrias at Hueco Tanks

Figure 183: Beatrice Morales, Irma Escontrias Sanchez, Mary Alice Tellez and Patricia Castaneda

Figure 184: Front Row: Mandy Uldock, Dahlia Gongora, Ralph and Yoly Pena Second Row: Jaime Sanchez, Patricia Castaneda, Mary Alice Tellez, Ruben Tellez, Jaime A. Sanchez, and Melissa Morales Third Row: Beatrice Morales, Mary and Paul Armendariz Last Row: Denisa Morales

Figure 185: Ruben and Mary Alice Tellez with Dahlia and Tony Gongora

Figure 186: Mary Alice Tellez, Dahlia Gongora, Irma Escontrias Sanchez

Figure 187: Beatrice Morales, Mary Alice Tellez, Patricia Castaneda, Irma Escontrias Sanchez, Cassandra Sanchez, Dahlia Gongora

Figure 188: Jaime Sanchez, Jaime A. Sanchez, Tony Gongora, Ruben Tellez and Dahlia Gongora

Figure 189: Dahlia Gongora and Irma Escontrias Sanchez

Figure 190: Patricia Castaneda, Beatrice Morales, Dahlia Gongora, Mary Alice Tellez, Irma Escontrias Sanchez

Figure 191: Cassandra Sanchez, Mary Alice Tellez, Jaime A. Sanchez, Patricia Castaneda, Beatrice Morales, Dahlia Gongora

Figure 192: Joshua Morales, Olivia Morales, Jaime A. Sanchez and Michelle Morales

Bernadette Sedillos Self / El Paso Times

TRAIL RIDE **Lower Valley resident Ernie Gomez,** far left, and Kimberly Dunn, 12, also of the Lower Valley, and others rode Saturday near the boundary of Hueco Tanks State Historical Site, after a trail ride from Hueco Tanks Ranch. The Escontrias Trail Ride, sponsored by the Cesar Serna Ranch and La Fe Clinic, raised money for Hueco Tanks. The ride was part of the Interpretive Fair events, which continue today at the park. Visitors can enter Hueco Tanks free today.

History will reign at Hueco Tanks fair

By Bernadette Sedillos Self
El Paso Times

▶ Trail ride details 2D

El Pasoans can enjoy pictograph and birding tours, ethnic dances, music, climbing demonstrations and other activities at the Hueco Tanks State Historic Site's Interpretive Fair on Saturday and Sunday at the site east of El Paso.

Also scheduled Saturday is the Escontrias Trail Ride, a fund-raiser for Hueco Tanks.

"This year, the event is going to be extra special because the Escontrias family, which originally owned the land, will bring old family photos and share some of their personal history and stories of growing up at the ranch," said Wanda Olszewski, Hueco Tanks superintendent.

The site was in the Silverio Escontrias family for many years (he died in the 1930s) and is world-renowned for its unique geology. The large rock formations attract climbers and boulderers from throughout the world, Olszewski said.

Hueco Tanks also is known for its pictographs, rock paintings made by Native American people. Some pictographs are more than 800 years old.

Guided pictograph tours will begin both days at 9:30 a.m.

It's believed that indigenous people may have lived in the Hueco Tanks area — which is a natural collection area for water — up to 12,000 years ago, Olszewski said.

The event includes numerous events for adults and children. Food, art and books will be available and environmental and cultural information booths also will have displays.

Those interested in seeing bird species can take the free tours that begin at 8 a.m.

Olszewski said it's important that the unique ecology, geology and archaeology of Hueco Tanks be carefully preserved so future generations of El Pasoans can enjoy the site.

Plant tours will be offered at 10 a.m. Olszewski said Hueco Tanks is the only home in the United States to a species of plant, colubrina stricta, that is thought to date from the Ice Age.

Olszewski said the site — it's no longer referred to as a park — is a precious natural, historical and cultural treasure.

"There are a couple of different aspects of its value to the community," Olszewski said. "It has very unique geology. It's a sanctuary for living things because of the water collection on the rocks, and it's really important for its archaeology, too.

"But I also think it is important because it holds stories about the human relationship to land," Olszewski added. "Standing beside some of these rocks and looking at a rock painting that was done 800 or 900 years ago — it's amazing."

Bernadette Sedillos Self may be reached at bself@elpasotimes.com; 546-6155.

Chapter 11
Our family

Figure 193: Carlos Escontrias with his four daughters: Mary Alice Tellez, Beatrice Morales, Patricia Castaneda and Irma Escontrias Sanchez

I know that my parent's biggest wish was that my sisters and I would love each other and stay close. I know so little about my father's family due to a break in his family. We are all working on fulfilling my parent's wishes. One of my nieces, Jessica Macias, even put together a yearly calendar so that we would know exactly what holidays we would be sharing and who would be in charge of that holiday. Staying close to your family takes work and commitment. I know that we are committed to sharing my parent's legacy through our children and our children's children.

Figure 194: Carlos and Maria Escontrias surrounded by their daughters Patricia Castaneda, Beatrice Morales, Irma Escontrias Sanchez and Mary Alice Tellez

Figure 195: Carlos and Maria Escontrias surrounded by their daughters Mary Alice Tellez, Irma Escontrias Sanchez, Beatrice Morales and Patricia Castaneda

Chapter 12
My Sisters' Recollections

Mary Alice Tellez

As I reflect back on my life, it gives me great pleasure and a sense of honor to have had two very wonderful and caring parents, Carlos and Maria De Jesus Escontrias, who also gifted me with three loving sisters, Bea, Patty and Irma. We grew up living in El Paso, Texas in the then small town of Socorro. When my grandmother Pilar lost her legs due to diabetes and was confined to a wheelchair, my mother became my grandmother's caregiver. I was twelve years old when my grandmother passed away. She was a very caring and giving person but was also strict in many ways

I never knew my grandfather. My grandparents Silverio and Pilar Escontrias proudly owned Hueco Tanks State Park located thirty-two miles northeast of El Paso in El Paso County aside from one additional home in Socorro. This eight hundred and sixty acre park is named for large natural rock basins or "huecos" that collect rain water for dwellers and travelers in the region of west Texas and was a frequent recreation site for many of my most cherished childhood memories. I remember when our families would gather for an all day picnic on Easter and other holidays.

I enjoyed the many trips we made to this park. My fondest memories include endless days of rock climbing, seeing the beautiful horses roaming the country side, cattle being branded, but mostly, enjoying the beauty and peacefulness one can find in such a remote and desolate region. I have always wondered why my grandfather chose that place to raise his eleven children. My Grandfather Silverio was a Texas Ranger for some years.

My grandfather and grandmother had a nature of caring and giving. My grandfather Silverio Escontrias also donated the land where the Socorro Mission La Purisima Catholic Church is situated. The church is located at 328 S. Nevarez Street in El Paso, Texas and is also where my husband Ruben and I were married. Our wedding reception was held in the thirty feet long by fifteen feet wide hallway of my parent's home which is located at 10409 Alameda. Also, my grandparents donated land with a decree stating that it be used for children's educational purposes only and is the present site of Escontrias Elementary School in the Socorro Independent School District.

It should come as no surprise that my father would follow somewhat in my grandfather's footsteps and be a "real Cowboy". I recall how awesome it seemed to me to see my own father participate in steer and calf roping at the Rough Riders. This brings back memories of days, back in the ranch, when we enjoyed swimming in the ponds along with the thrill of getting each other wet with our canteens. The water in the canteens always seemed very good and very cold.

My father, Carlos Escontrias was a very quiet person whom anyone could depend on for help when needed. He passionately loved my mother for many years. They shared fifty-six years of wedded bliss.

At our home, we had horses, cows, roosters, chickens and rabbits. We had apricot trees, pear trees and pecan trees. We also had fifty acres of cotton. This is where I learned firsthand the difficult task of picking cotton. We had a very deep well from which we would irrigate the cotton fields. I feel that my three sisters and myself have been so blessed to have shared such beautiful moments that we will forever cherish. I think back warmheartedly of milking the cows because I know I will probably never have another opportunity to do that again. The home where we all "grew up" is more than one hundred years old. As for the holidays, Christmas was the most important and best celebrated holiday for it was a day of family togetherness and giving thanks to God Almighty. Our Mother had a very unique manner of decorating the Christmas tree so beautifully it would make one feel so warm and filled with love and happiness. We would want to spend as much time as one could in that special room. My sisters and I waited eagerly looking forward to the Christmas holiday.

I also want to say that when I met Ruben Tellez, my husband, was when I went horseback riding on my Dad's awesome horse, Barrozo. We had gone to the levy and I saw this young man staring at me. Of course that thrilled me. We eventually got married and my husband, Ruben, would make the comment that it was not I he had fallen in love with; it was the beautiful horse, Barrozo, That comment doesn't bother me because we have spent forty years of wedded bliss. We are the proud parents of two wonderful sons, Ruben Jr. and Ralph. Ruben is married to Missy and they have blessed us with three wonderful grandsons named Julian, Josiah and Elijah who mean the world to me.

My Dad and Mom were my life and I will never forget what thoughtful and caring people they were. The love they gave and showed my sisters and myself will be in our hearts forever. We were very blessed and ever thankful to God to have given us such great parents...Carlos and Maria Escontrias. I would like to add that my sisters, Beatrice, Patty and little sister Irma are awesome and I will love them forever. I am so proud to be part of the Escontrias legacy.

In ending, I recollect back to my father and would like to tenderly articulate that he was a "true cowboy". He was the last of the breed who participated in the Lower Valley Rough Riders Association in which he performed calf roping and head and heel roping. It was an immense experience of mine to eyewitness all my father loved doing. And last but not least, I want to say that my mother and father loved to dance and were excellent country western dancers.

Beatrice Morales

My name is Beatrice Escontrias Morales and my parents were Charlie and Mary Escontrias. I have three sisters whose names are Mary Alice Tellez, Patty Castaneda, and Irma A. Sanchez, who by the way is the guest speaker every year during October for the Hueco

Tanks Interpretive Fair.

When I was a child growing up, I remember my parents and my Grandmother were living at the old Escontrias home. I did not have the honor to meet my Grandfather, because he had passed away a long time ago. My dad's brother, Ramon lived next door to us and at that time my Grandmother was a diabetic and had her legs amputated during her long illness. My Uncle Ramon would come to the house to give her a shot almost every day. My Grandmother was a great person and adapted to pain all her life. My younger sister Patty always sat by my grandmother's wheelchair taking care of her. I remember when it was the day for the farmers all around this town of Socorro. Their patron saint was "**San Isidro**" and everyone would come to our home and there would be lots of food and refreshments for everyone. It was so beautiful and they all would carry our patron saint to different ranches, but ours was one of the first they would stop by. I recall thinking about Grandma Pilar and Mom and all the people who helped out could accomplish feeding all these people of all ages. This yearly event was so touching, so beautiful and so heartwarming.

I remember my father, Charlie Escontrias was a calf roper and we would all get in the truck and my sister and cousins would ride the horses while in the trailer. This was risky business, but we never saw the danger; we were just enjoying life to the fullest. The Escontrias family was full of life and some of the adventures were just so incredible, we could not believe it.

I also remember our days at Hueco Tanks. I think I was the tomboy in the family because I would horseback ride a lot during my childhood years. I remember back at Hueco Tanks there were a lot of cowboys everywhere. I remember seeing horses and calves getting branded with the SE brand. My Uncle Ramon would make the best beef jerky in the world. We would all go mountain climbing and see breathtaking scenery along the rocks, wild landscaping, waterfalls, deer, rabbits and snakes along the paths.

I also remember all the Easter picnics we had with all our cousins and family at Hueco Tanks. Playing baseball, mountain climbing, Easter hunts, and eating all day long. What wonderful memories we all had. We would see all the artifacts on the rocks everywhere and we were told a story about one of the rocks having a big treasure of gold, but no one ever found it. We were told that an Indian found it and was killed by someone that wanted that treasure as well. It seems no one ever got possession of it. My father, Charlie Escontrias, the youngest sibling of the

Escontrias family knew more or less where the spot was that contained the treasure, but we never found it either.

The memories will live on and on and we will tell our children all the wonderful stories our parents told us about the past and they as well will tell their children and so on and so on. The Escontrias Family is a legacy, and it should be taken to the fullest with all the history of these beautiful and wonderful people. I am so proud to have had two wonderful parents like Carlos and Maria Escontrias.

Patricia Castaneda

When my sister Irma first told me that she was going to be writing a book about the history of the

Escontrias family I was truly excited. I feel like our family is well deserving of a book in their honor. However, when she asked me and my two other sisters to write a recollection of our family I wondered what I was going to write. After giving it some thought I started writing and could not stop. As I wrote I relived my childhood days which were so wonderful. The stories you will read in this recollection were so real it was like I was reliving them all over again. I can still see the beautiful flowers in the garden. I can hear the horses neighing in the corral and the chirp of birds flying over the rooftop. I want to thank my sister for giving me this opportunity to relive the best years a child could ask for. The following is the end result of my thoughts.

I have sweet recollections of my childhood at the Escontrias home. As I grew up as a child, a very happy one at that, I had no clue that my last name (Escontrias) was so famous. My parents always taught me to treat everyone with love and respect no matter how much or how little that person might have had. I was a daughter to a wonderful couple – Carlos and Maria Escontrias…a granddaughter to Silverio and Pilar Escontrias…and a sister to Mary Alice, Beatrice, and Irma Escontrias. Never in my wildest dreams did I ever imagine that my grandparents would be in the

Texas Historical Encyclopedias or that the very first school in Socorro School District would be named after them. I also never knew that I would work in that very same school for several years and those would be the happiest working days of my life. All I knew at that time that I was Patricia Escontrias and Pilar Escontrias was affectionately known to me as Grandma.

My belief as a child was that all homes had the same things that were in our house. The blue velvet sofas, the beautiful embroidered maroon pillows on the sofas, the antique bedroom sets whose drawers were made of cedar wood....I just thought that they were ordinary things. I guess I never knew better because I never remember sleeping over at a friend's house. I preferred staying at home or with my cousins at their houses. I enjoyed my home very much. The front porch was my favorite. I remember spending a lot of time with my dolls there. Flowers of every color bloomed in the yard. Cottonwood trees and those beautiful cat tail bushes sat on the lawn. So much shade, so much fragrance, so much beauty. I loved my home, my family and especially my childhood.

Grandma Pilar Escontrias was a wonderful person. She never was able to see any of us sisters because diabetes had caused her to become blind. That dreadful disease also caused gangrene to claim both her legs. So I remember my grandma in a wheelchair all her life. She did have a bad habit though. She loved to smoke. We felt like she probably would never listen to us to stop smoking so we let her. My grandmother required twenty four hour care and my mother did that for her unconditionally. My mother was a rather small person and grandma was a little on the heavy side. You can imagine the toll it took on my mother's back picking her up from the bed to the wheelchair, back to bed, and so forth. However, my mother never complained.

My mother nursed my grandmother back to health when she had her legs amputated. Grandma fell off the bed one time causing a rather large wound to her head and there was my mother taking care of her once more. My grandmother dealt with so much illness that it is hard to believe what finally claimed her life was pneumonia. Grandma was a rather stubborn woman who did not take no for an answer. She insisted on being wheeled out to the lawn on the feast of San Isidro to enjoy the festivities. All it took was a small breeze to make her become ill. It did not take long to develop into pneumonia and she passed away. She died in the month of May. I will never forget that because she had promised to make me a birthday party just a few days away from her passing. I loved

Grandma……she was stubborn, always in a smoke-filled room, but otherwise a very happy woman.

The feast of San Isidro was held once a year to celebrate the season of the crops. Farmers would get into a horse-drawn cart and take the patron saint of San Isidro with them from farm to farm. I remember the table with the white tablecloth that awaited them. On the table were what I recall as wine and "viscochitos" (Mexican cookies). All would enjoy the refreshments and praise the saint for another year of good agriculture. Then they would leave and head off to the next farm. Thank goodness I did not like wine then or they would have been out of luck by the time they got there.

Even though my father came from a very large family, eleven in total, I hardly knew any of them. I remember my Uncle Santiago (Jim) and Uncle Ramon with extreme fondness. I also remember my Aunt Manuela quite well. The rest of the family was either already deceased or had chosen to stay away from our family. It seemed that when my Grandma Pilar died so did the family unity. It probably never bothered me because my mother's side of the family was very family-oriented and that side of the family made up for our loss. They loved coming to the house and my parents always made them all feel so welcome they did not want to leave. To this day I feel we have remained close all because we were taught at an early age that family ties were important.

Grandpa Silverio was a great person whom I did not have the pleasure of meeting. He died when my father was about nine years old. He was a Texas Ranger and owned a lot of land here in Socorro. He donated the land for the first school to be built, donated land for the cemetery at La Purisima Church and was truly a generous man. It was through talking to my mother and father that I learned a little about his death. Apparently in those days men carried their guns in their holsters. Some of my uncles were sitting around a campfire when an argument between two of them started. It ended when one brother shot his own brother dead. It took a tremendous toll on my grandfather and his health started to fail. He died a short time later probably due to a broken heart.

My Uncle Ramon and Aunt Chavela were the ones that remained the closest to my parents. They lived in the home next door about a couple of acres away. Cotton crops grew between both homes. When I was a child I thought that my uncle was Roy Rogers and my aunt was Dale Evans. They really resembled them. They were always dressed in western attire and I can remember them being on horseback pretty regularly. They had two daughters named Yolanda and Yvonne. It seemed like we were always together. My cousin Yoly was a barrel racer and Yvonne just liked hanging around mostly with my sister Beatrice. They were fun to be around but they moved to California and we kind of lost track of them for a while.

One story that remains deeply in my mind is about Yolanda, the older of the two cousins. One day Yolanda had had a disagreement with her parents and became very upset. She decided to come over to our house and talk to my mother about the incident. My mother, being the type of person she was, calmed her down and gave her some good advice about being patient with her mom and dad. When Yolanda finally decided to go home it was already dark outside. She started walking and heard a noise and raced back to our house after becoming startled. My mom reassured her that it was probably the horses that had hit the trough so she left again. Once more she heard the same noise and again came back to our house. Again, my mother reassured her that it was nothing to be afraid of so she left again. However this time when she was halfway home we heard a loud screeching scream. My mom and her parents ran to see what was happening and Yolanda was on the ground. She had fainted. Apparently she had seen a ball of fire following her and when she screamed it vanished. To this day it is believed that the devil had paid her a little visit. That was enough to make her become different with her parents. My mother was never paid a visit from Yolanda again.

Things were so simple then. I remember the crisp linen on the beds after the sheets had been hung out on the clothesline. I can still feel the soft breeze entering through open windows that caused the curtains to sway ever so gently. I can smell the homemade tortillas that Mom had been busy preparing for our dinner. I can hear the sounds of the peacocks venturing around the grounds. I can taste the fruit from our various trees which included pear, peach, apricot trees that grew along the ditch which brought irrigation water to the surrounding crops of cotton. I can hear the sound of the crop duster plane that flew so low overhead I was certain that it was going to hit our roof one day. I can still see the pecan grove encircled by a corral which was the home to several horses, cows and even some miniature calves.

I loved thunderstorms during the summer months. The thunder seemed to rumble endlessly and the lightning strikes seemed to be right outside your door. My mother was terrified of lightning so there she was scrambling to cover all mirrors with sheets. She did this to prevent lightning from coming in and bouncing off the mirror. I never knew if this could really happen or if it was just another old wives' tale. However my mother sure did take it seriously. She would actually pull out a rosary and start praying. I, on the other hand, would tell God to send more thunder by saying "aprietale Tata Diosito" and my mother would get furious at me. I thought it was funny then but now that I am grown I can actually feel her fear. When the storm was over, we went out to play in the puddles and make mud pies. We actually used an old horse trailer and set it up as a bakery. We "sold" mud cakes, mud pies, or mud cupcakes. All of these activities were innocent fun. One thing for sure, we never had any customers.

My sisters and I played hide and seek but if we dared play inside the house we were thrown out. A peach basket served as a basketball rim. Climbing trees and roof tops were fun and a way of getting away from the chubby ones that could not climb as well. Our seesaw was just a plain board placed on the fence. Our mother would prepare a big pan of steamed rice with cinnamon and milk and we would go for a long walk and sit under this big tree and have a picnic with this treat. We found so many ways to amuse ourselves and it was all so much fun.

As a child I do not recall going to see a doctor other than for nosebleeds and deep cuts. My mother always used home remedies for our aches and pains. She had some little plants growing in the front yard. It was called "hierba buena" which means "good plant". She would boil the plant and add sugar and it would cure stomach aches and other ailments. She also had a live plant called "savila" that was used for burns, actual toothaches, or rash. Then there was the infamous "Lavativa" which is the Spanish word for enema. This would cure anything according to my mother. It seemed like it would cure depression if my mother said it would. Ask any family member about this famous little gadget and they have some stories of their own, most of them hilarious.

My father had several pecan trees. When Thanksgiving came around we would pick the pecans and shell them. We would eat them just like that or we would save some for one of the famous dishes my mother prepared. One dish contained apples, pecans, sugar and hard to believe but mayonnaise was one of the main ingredients. I have to admit it was delicious.

Tradition was a big thing at the Escontrias home. We tried our very best to all eat together at suppertime. I have to admit my sister would con me into washing the dishes when it was her turn for a measly quarter. Try telling a kid that today. They will give a turn and march right outside the door.

My parents were very family oriented. It seemed like there was always a gathering at home. It was my cousins' favorite place to visit. If we weren't "swimming" in the ditch we were picking apricots off the trees. Of course we were daring sometimes too. We liked to chase the chickens, go searching for the eggs they had laid or just run after each other screaming like crazy people. There were no neighbors around to complain so we had lots of fun.

One of the best foods I ever ate at home was the "cabrito" (baby goat) that was cooked in an outside pit. A rather deep hole was made and lots of dried branches were placed inside. The meat would cook for hours sometimes overnight. All the family would come over and we would have a feast. The parties would continue into the late hours of the night. That family tradition was memorable.

Our home had weeping willow trees along the ditch behind our house and sometimes we would pretend to be acrobats and swing from ditch bank to ditch bank. Those weeping willows served another purpose though. When we had finally gotten on my mother's last nerve she would cut one of the branches off the tree and threaten to whip us with it. We would find that adrenalin rush and run like the dickens in the opposite direction. She would yell at us to stop and that would just make us run faster. She knew that when we got hungry we would return home. By that time our dear mother had forgotten all about it. (Thank God)

Horses played an important role in the Escontrias home. For as long as I can remember the corral was always home to many horses. My dad was a true cowboy. He competed in many rodeos. He was an excellent calf roper. It seemed like we were always at the rodeos watching him compete. Other times we just enjoyed being home where life was truly wonderful.

My parents always had dogs around. They were helpful because they served as watch dogs to protect the animals. One of the dogs that I will never forget was a collie that looked just like Lassie. He followed my sister Mary Alice around all the time. Apparently my sister would get home from school and the first thing she would do was to kick off her boots and leave them lying where they fell. That dog would pick them up and take them to her. Unfortunately he crossed a busy street to welcome my sister from school when he was hit by a car and killed. That is when I felt like it was not worth it to get so attached to an animal that would leave you so suddenly.

My sister Beatrice loved to ride horses. She was even thrown from one and she took a rather bad knock on the head. When they ran to pick her up she had trouble with her vision. She became blind for a little while but her vision did return. That did not stop her from getting back on those horses. What I really enjoyed seeing was the wiglet on her head to portray long hair going up and down, up and down, up and down with the trotting of the horse. You could pick her out on a field of horseback riders.

I am ten years older than my youngest sister Irma. When she was born she took the place of my dolls. I played with her instead. I changed her diapers and just took over. In fact, one day we had just come home from somewhere, and I decided to run down the hall with her. My mother's house had a very long corridor right in the center of the house. When I started running I did not notice that the telephone cord was stretched across the hallway. I tripped and my little sister flew out of my arms and went sliding what seemed to be the end of the hallway. I screamed at the top of my lungs that I had just killed my little sister and I was afraid to go see the result of my carelessness. After slowly uncovering the blankets, I found a giggling baby that seemed to tell me "That was fun, let's do it again".

Then there was the infamous "Felix". I never even knew his last name. He was the hired hand that lived there at the Escontrias farm. He had a little adobe room that was attached to some other rooms that my dad used for storage. I remember him making himself food over a little campfire or making coffee from a "petre" pot. I actually joined him a lot of times for dinner. Those were the days when you trusted everyone and you never thought people could be evil.

Even though he was very good to all the family members he left the house one day without telling anyone. He left with many of our grandparent's belongings. He took guns, branding irons, etc. These things could never be replaced. This was a good lesson for us, never judge a book by its cover. I would never have imagined that he could be capable of being a thief. He left back to Mexico and we never saw or heard from him again.

I am the proud grandmother to several grandchildren and this is the best opportunity to reveal my childhood life. I am guilty of not sitting the oldest ones down and sharing my history with them. It seems like we just do not take the time to do this because the children have their own interests. This book will be the best way to tell them stories about our family. They will also find out the sincere, sometimes funny and wonderful experiences that their grandmother had as a child. Here are a couple that I can still remember as if it were today.

My mother used to dress me and my sister Bea alike almost all the time. For Christmas we received the same gifts. One Christmas, we both got dolls and we named them Cindy and Lindy. We were playing in the front porch one day with our dolls. I still do not know why but I was playing with matches. I would light the match and just blow it out (some fun, huh?) Well my mother called us to come and eat lunch and I decided I would light just one more match and I thought I had blown it out and threw it. When we finished lunch we went back to our dolls and to my amazement the match had landed on Cindy (Beatrice's doll) and her face was badly burned. Beatrice started to cry. She was furious at me. I offered to give her my doll that was a duplicate of hers but she would not hear of it. Instead we just bandaged Cindy up and continued to play. I am so lucky it was only the doll that got burnt and not the house.

I have mentioned in my recollection of the beautiful flowers my mother had growing in the garden. In the month of May, it was a custom to go every day to our Church and offer fresh flowers to the Virgin Mary. My mother would dress us in our First Communion dresses and take us to church every day with our freshly picked flowers. We would place them on the altar. I can still smell the aroma of all those flowers. Many young girls participated in this tradition and it was a beautiful opportunity to dress up for the occasion.

Mom was big on religion. She dressed us in our Sunday best clothes each and every weekend to go to Mass. She expected us to be on our best behavior. Right before Mass was going to end, the priest would make announcements. At that time parents were reminded to take their children to catechism at this old lady's house. I did not like to go, so it was during the announcements that I would take that opportunity to get my mom's attention to distract her from hearing the announcements. I quickly found out that my distraction did not work because she took me and my sisters anyway. This little old lady was strict and before we knew it we were ready to make the sacrament of First Communion.

La Purisima Catholic Church had a priest by the name of Father Zuniga. It seemed like he had been there forever. I remember when the priest only faced the congregation during the homily. The rest of the mass was directed to the altar. Boy, have things changed. Anyway, my mother invited Father Zuniga on Saturday mornings for breakfast. He ate sunny side eggs, bacon, and what seemed like a tower of toast with such enthusiasm that I usually wanted some of the same when he left. There was a downfall to inviting him to our house. He would pile me and my sisters in his car to take us to the church for more catechism. We would go to other girls' houses and pick them up so they could go too. He would honk many times until the girls would come out. Even if we tried to ignore his honking so that we would not have to go he honked even more. We finally would give up and get in the car. I have to admit he was not the best driver and he was lucky they did not give tickets at that time for driving so slow. It seemed like an eternity to get to the church especially because he drove so recklessly. If memory serves me well, we landed in a ditch one time so that didn't make it any easier to want to go next time. But in spite of that, Mom always made sure we went. I wonder how we all did not become nuns with as much time as we spent at the church.

My mother had a great sense of humor. She thought she was doing us sisters a favor by taking us to get perms in our hair right before picture day at school. I have tried to destroy my pictures but have not been able to locate them. Aside from that, my mother always had us in the latest fashion, whether it be western attire or go-go boots (white with little tassels). Like I said I loved her sense of humor.

In coming to Mom's defense I do remember my sister Mary Alice wearing a poodle skirt when I started in the first grade. I remember because I held on to that skirt for dear life. I had not made any friends so I hung around with her. She was not too happy about the whole arrangement. Gradually I made my own friends and she could act like the big girl on campus once again.

There was a mischievous side of me as a young girl. I once got on one of the horses without permission. Everything was going well until something spooked the horse. It started running wildly in the corral. The corral had a bunch of pecan trees and the branches in some of the trees were very low. I remember having to duck to keep the branches from scratching my face. All the time I was screaming bloody murder. After what seemed like a long time, my father finally came out of the house to my rescue. He could not stop laughing at me but he finally was able to corral the horse into a corner and I was able to get off. I never got on another horse again.

We had a washer with a wringer attached on top. (This was a top of the line washer in those days) Well I never said I was the smartest in the family. I had a packet of red Kool aid in my pocket. I went to the washroom and I thought it would be fun to get a sock that was being washed in the washing machine and put it through the wringer. I put it in too far and my whole hand went through the wringer. When it got to my forearm the wringer started making some weird noises and so did I. I screamed at the top of my lungs. The water was coming out of the washer and landing on my pocket. When my mother finally found me she thought I was bleeding. It was the Kool aid that had seeped through my pocket. Then she saw my arm and hit an emergency release on the machine. I took out my arm and the next thing I felt was a large steak on my bruised arm. That felt good but it also made me very hungry. She did not ask me to help her with the laundry for a long time. Wonder why?

The Fourth of July was always fun at our house. Since we lived out of the city limits, all of our family would come and pop their fireworks at our house. I remember these chasers that would always come after my sister Mary Alice. I liked the black cats because you could make them last so long...........one at a time........it seemed liked there were thousands of them to pop before the night was over. As I have mentioned previously my mother had chickens so we would take away the eggs they had just laid and put fireworks on them and make them explode. We also got coke bottles and did the same. I am so surprised we never got injured or got into big trouble with my Mom for having done these daring things. The chickens did not like us much but they paid the price too when we felt like eating fried chicken.

I remember my childhood injuries. I once cut my hand with a glass. We had a water pump outside and I kept on filling the glass with water and then spilling the water for no apparent reason. Our "nanny" came outside and caught me doing this and asked me to stop. She was worried that I would cut myself and there was no way of getting to a doctor since both my parents were out of town. Sure enough I fell with the glass and got a huge gash on my hand. She stopped the bleeding but I had to wait until the next day to go to the doctor when my parents came back. The doctor looked at my cut and had to scrub it with a scouring pad to get rid of the dried flesh and to make it bleed again. Then he applied several stitches. I hate to admit this but a few days later I fell again and reopened it. I feel sorry for my parents and the things I made them go through.

My mother was such a generous person not only to her own family but with total strangers. Homeless people came by pretty frequently to our house asking for food or money. My mother would go inside the house and prepare a burrito or a sandwich for them and give them some money for the road. She never saw the danger in being a Good Samaritan. She took in stray dogs and cats and even nursed a little deer when it was separated from its mother. She would help anyone that needed clothing, money, or transportation to the store or to the bank. Even after she passed away my sister kept on paying for the Miracle Network for Kids that she was so proud to be a member of. That was the trend of the Escontrias family….generous, sympathetic, loving and respectful.

All in all, life was good at the Escontrias home. Simple people with simple pleasures. I am blessed to have had the childhood that I had. I just wish that my own children and grandchildren would have had the same opportunities I did. Older people were admired and respected. Even though I feel like my own children had a good childhood I would have loved for them to have the same experiences that I did. Those memories will stay forever in my heart.

CHAPTER 13
HUECO TANKS STAFF
RECOLLECTIONS

The Escontrias Family Legacy
at Hueco Tanks State Park and Historic Site

-Wanda Olszewski

The story of human relationship to the land of Hueco Tanks spans over 10,000 years. Within that story, the Escontrias Family holds a special place. The Escontrias

Ranch (1898-1956) was a unique period in the history of Hueco Tanks and the region, and also was a link between very different eras. In the time before ranching began there, Hueco Tanks was still considered a wild place; its attraction as a water source drew passing travelers, but they did not stay long. Silverio Escontrias and his family dared to make the place a home. By the time the area now known as Hueco Tanks State Park and Historic Site passed into other hands over fifty years later, "modern" times had fully arrived and the "Wild West" was something people sought to recreate.

The Escontrias Family were also the first to manage several aspects of Hueco Tanks that would be of increasing importance in years to come, such as its attractions as both a cultural site and a recreational area. The area's increasing popularity as a day trip and picnic area did not come without challenges to the ranching operations. However, the Escontrias' awareness of the site's amazing pictographs and openness to those with interest in them led to lasting benefits. For example, a visit Forrest Kirkland (a commercial artist from Dallas) made to the ranch in 1939 resulted in his creation of over 1,000 watercolor recordings of the pictograph images he and his wife Lula found. This early inventory remains an invaluable record of the images as they were seen seventy years ago, and still serves as the basis for the pictograph nomenclature used at Hueco Tanks today.

Although Silverio, his wife Pilar and many of their eleven children moved to a new home in Socorro so that the children could go to school, the family still operated the ranch at Hueco Tanks and spent much time there. The memories of those days are the source of the best stories the family still shares through several generations. I was lucky enough to hear some of these from Carlos "Charlie" Escontrias, his wife Mary and their family.

Charlie Escontrias, Silverio's youngest son, was a soft-spoken man with genteel, traditional manners and a streak of playful humor that could take one by pleasant surprise. My favorite memory of him involves a visit I made to the historic family home in Socorro, together with a Texas Parks and Wildlife filming crew, to interview him and other family for the park's orientation video. The powerful emotional ties Mr. Escontrias had to the subject led some family members to think that our attempt to interview him would fail.

At first I thought so, too. But out of nowhere came an idea for a question.

"Tell me about your favorite horse," I said.

There was a moment of silence. Then he turned to one of his daughters, and asked her to get his hat.

The meaning of this wasn't clear to me at first, but then they explained; this meant he was going to talk. The hat was brought and placed on his head, and he did.

For various reasons, that piece was not included in the short park video, and the Escontrias Family was represented with other footage. However, it stays in my memory along with the stories he told: of chasing deer on horseback and lassoing their antlers as roping practice, or of riding his horse across the top of the rock and cement dam that stretches across Mescalero Canyon, defying the treacherous drop on either side.

Although he was already in a wheelchair when I met him, I came to see within the soft-spoken man this brave and even daredevil youth of his past, always able to make me smile in surprise. Although Charlie Escontrias has passed, at Hueco Tanks he still lives, in the spirit of the place, in the photos of him with his horse, and in the stories we pass on to visitors.

Charlie's wife Mary is also missed. She was a person who possessed incredible beauty in both person and spirit. I remember most her persuasive power to draw people in- even those she had just met- to the house for a meal or into laughter with at her something that was said. In Mary and Charlie, their daughter Irma Escontrias Sanchez and all of the family members today, one can feel the closeness, hospitality and pride which have doubtless always been traditional hallmarks of the Escontrias character.

The family's willingness to share their history has been an ongoing gift to Hueco Tanks, leading its visitors to a greater understanding of the site and the history of our area.

Irma Escontrias Sanchez speaking at the Hueco Tanks Interpretive Fair, 2004

To today's visitors, the Escontrias Family and the "ranch house" home represent a past both romantic and rugged. Though a seeming contradiction, this connection is natural. The ranch was at once the last gasp of the expansive "Wild West" at Hueco Tanks and the beginning of modern times, in which the site has increasingly become a rare natural and cultural island rapidly approached by development. For that reason, visitors to Hueco Tanks will always enjoy and benefit from the glimpse into history that only the Escontrias Family can provide.

Chapter 14
Escontrias Family Photos

Figure 196: Chavela Escontrias

Figure 197: Charlie Armendariz

Figure 198: Manuela Apodaca

Figure 199: Pete Armendariz

Figure 200: Escontrias Family Photo

Figure 201: Pilar Escontrias and Family

Figure 202: Carlos Escontrias and Paul Armendariz

Figure 203: Escontrias family ranch photo

Figure 204: Escontrias family ranch photo

Figure 205: Escontrias family ranch photo

Figure 206: Escontrias ranch family photo

Figure 207: Escontrias family photo

Figure 208: Escontrias Ranch

Figure 209: Branding cattle with the SE bar at the Escontrias Ranch

Figure 210: Pilar Escontrias at the Socorro Farm

Figure 211: Escontrias family photo

Figure 212: Photo found which lists Juan Escontrias on caption

Figure 213: Photo found in Escontrias records possibly tied to school

Hueco Tanks Pictures

Figure 214: Beautiful Hueco Tanks

Figure 215: Another view

Figure 216: Hueco Tanks

Figure 217: Hueco Tanks

Figure 218: Hueco Tanks

Figure 219: Hueco Tanks

Figure 220: Hueco Tanks

Figure 221: Hueco Tanks

Figure 222: Hueco Tanks

Figure 223: Hueco Tanks

Figure 224: Hueco Tanks

Figure 225: Hueco Tanks

Figure 226: Hueco Tanks

Figure 227: Hueco Tanks

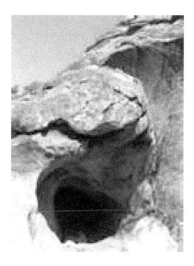

Figure 228: Hueco Tanks

Figure 229: C. Escontrias remains carved on the rocks of Hueco Tanks

Figure 230: Hueco Tanks pictograph reprinted with permission from the collections of the Texas Parks and Wildlife Department

Figure 231: Hueco Tanks pictograph reprinted with permission from the collection of the Texas Parks and Wildlife

Figure 232: Hueco Tanks pictograph reprinted with permission from the collection of the Texas Parks and Wildlife Department

Figure 233: Hueco Tanks pictograph reprinted with permission from the collections of the Texas Parks and Wildlife Department

Figure 234: Hueco Tanks pictograph reprinted with permission from the collections of the Texas Parks and Wildlife Department

Figure 235: Hueco Tanks pictograph reprinted with permission from the collections of the Texas Parks and Wildlife Department

Figure 236: Hueco Tanks pictograph reprinted with permission from the collections of the Texas Parks and Wildlife Department

Figure 237: Hueco Tanks pictograph reprinted with permission from the collections of the Texas Parks and Wildlife

Figure 238: Hueco Tanks pictograph reprinted with permission from the collections of the Texas Parks and Wildlife Department

Figure 239: Hueco Tanks pictograph reprinted with permission from the collections of the Texas Parks and Wildlife Department

Figure 240: Hueco Tanks pictograph reprinted with permission from the collections of the Texas Parks and Wildlife Department

Figure 241: Hueco Tanks picture reprinted with permission from the collections of the Texas Parks and Wildlife Department

Figure 242: Hueco Tanks picture reprinted with permission from
the collections of the Texas Parks and Wildlife Department

Figure 243: Hueco Tanks picture reprinted with permission from
the collections of the Texas Parks and Wildlife Department

Figure 244: Hueco Tanks picture reprinted with permission from the collections of the Texas Parks and Wildlife Department

Figure 245: Hueco Tanks picture reprinted with permission from the collections of the Texas Parks and Wildlife Department

Figure 246: Hueco Tanks picture reprinted with permission from the collections of the Texas Parks and Wildlife Department

Figure 247: Hueco Tanks picture reprinted with permission from the collections of the Texas Parks and Wildlife Department

Figure 248: Hueco Tanks picture reprinted with permission from the collections of the Texas Parks and Wildlife Department

Figure 249: Hueco Tanks picture reprinted with permission from the collections of the Texas Parks and Wildlife Department

Figure 250: Hueco Tanks picture reprinted with permission from the collections of the Texas Parks and Wildlife Department

Figure 251: Hueco Tanks picture reprinted with permission from the collections of the Texas Parks and Wildlife Department

Figure 252: Hueco Tanks picture reprinted with permission from the collections of the Texas Parks and Wildlife Department

Figure 253: Hueco Tanks picture reprinted with permission from the collections of the Texas Parks and Wildlife Department

Figure 254: Hueco Tanks picture reprinted with permission from the collections of the Texas Parks and Wildlife Department

Figure 255: Hueco Tanks picture reprinted with permission from the collections of the Texas Parks and Wildlife Department

Figure 256: Hueco Tanks picture reprinted with permission from the collections of the Texas Parks and Wildlife Department

Figure 257: Hueco Tanks picture reprinted with permission from the collections of the Texas Parks and Wildlife Department

Figure 258: Hueco Tanks picture reprinted with permission from the collections of the Texas Parks and Wildlife Department

Figure 259: Hueco Tanks picture reprinted with permission from the collections of the Texas Parks and Wildlife Department

Figure 260: Hueco Tanks picture reprinted with permission from the collections of the Texas Parks and Wildlife Department

Figure 261: Hueco Tanks wildlife reprinted with permission from the collections of the Texas Parks and Wildlife Department

Figure 262: Hueco Tanks wildlife reprinted with permission from the collections of the Texas Parks and Wildlife Department

Figure 263: Hueco Tanks wildlife reprinted with permission from the collections of the Texas Parks and Wildlife Department

Figure 264: Hueco Tanks wildlife reprinted with permission from the collections of the Texas Parks and Wildlife Department

Figure 265: Hueco Tanks wildlife reprinted with permission from the collections of the Texas Parks and Wildlife Department

Figure 266: Hueco Tanks wildlife reprinted with permission from the collections of the Texas Parks and Wildlife Department

Figure 267: Hueco Tanks wildlife reprinted with permission from the collections of the Texas Parks and Wildlife Department

Figure 268: Hueco Tanks wildlife reprinted with permission from the collections of the Texas Parks and Wildlife Department

Figure 269: Hueco Tanks wildlife reprinted with permission from the collections of the Texas Parks and Wildlife Department

Figure 270: Hueco Tanks wildlife reprinted with permission from the collections of the Texas Parks and Wildlife Department

Figure 271: Hueco Tanks wildlife reprinted with permission from the collections of the Texas Parks and Wildlife Department

Ending thoughts

All of us have a story to tell. I wish I had written this book when my parents were still alive. This book has enabled me to leave a small legacy dedicated to my parents, Carlos and Maria Escontrias and my grandparents Silverio and Pilar Escontrias. Now, our future generations can use this information as a stepping stone for their own stories. It is my hope that our stories will not die and will live on. I know that each descendant of the Escontrias family will also leave a lasting legacy for generations to come.

I encourage everyone to write your own story and leave a trail of memories for your own family. Although all we have left to visit is a cemetery, I know I have four angels in heaven smiling down with pride and happiness in the family they have left behind who love each other.

**Figure 272: Carlos and Maria Escontrias –
May you Rest in Peace!**

**Figure 273: Silverio and Pilar Escontrias –
May You Rest In Peace!**

ABOUT THE AUTHOR

Irma Escontrias Sanchez was the first person in her family to attain a college degree. Irma graduated from the University of Texas at El Paso with a Bachelor of Science degree in Education. Irma taught for twenty nine years before retiring and enjoyed her journey as a Reading teacher for Ysleta Middle School, V.W. Miller Intermediate, Valley View Middle School and Desert View Middle School. She then worked as an ESL teacher at Desert View Middle School. Irma ended her teaching career at Desert View Middle School as an AVID Coordinator. In 2010, Desert View Middle School became a National AVID Demonstration School through the hard work of the entire staff and faculty.

Irma has been bestowed the honor of Teacher of the Year at Valley View Middle School as well as Teacher of the Year twice at Desert View Middle School. She also made the Top Ten Teacher of the Year finalist list for the Ysleta Independent School District and was recognized by The El Paso County Council IRA by being awarded the Outstanding Teacher of Reading Award. In 2014, she was bestowed the honor of receiving the BEEMS Bilingual Advocate of the Year award.

Irma has a wonderful husband, Jaime Sanchez, who has supported Irma in everything she has wanted to do throughout her life. Irma also has two children, Cassandra and Jaime, who have made her a proud Mother. Irma wanted Cassie and Jaime to know about their amazing family. Irma currently works as a consultant for Renaissance Learning, Inc. as well as a Book Representative for Opal Booz & Associates.

Irma hopes that this book will inspire everyone to write their own life story.

INDEX

CPSIA information can be obtained
at www.ICGtesting.com
Printed in the USA
BVHW070856060319
541923BV00011B/319/P